PABLO ESCOBAR

The True Story of Cocaine King

MAFIA LIBRARY

© **Copyright 2024 - All rights reserved.**

The content contained within this book may not be reproduced, duplicated or transmitted without direct written permission from the author or the publisher.

Under no circumstances will any blame or legal responsibility be held against the publisher, or author, for any damages, reparation, or monetary loss due to the information contained within this book, either directly or indirectly.

Legal Notice:

This book is copyright protected. It is only for personal use. You cannot amend, distribute, sell, use, quote or paraphrase any part, or the content within this book, without the consent of the author or publisher.

Disclaimer Notice:

Please note the information contained within this document is for educational and entertainment purposes only. All effort has been executed to present accurate, up to date, reliable, complete information. No warranties of any kind are declared or implied. Readers acknowledge that the author is not engaged in the rendering of legal, financial, medical or professional advice. The content within this book has been derived from various sources. Please consult a licensed professional before attempting any techniques outlined in this book.

By reading this document, the reader agrees that under no circumstances is the author responsible for any losses, direct or indirect, that are incurred as a result of the use of the information contained within this document, including, but not limited to, errors, omissions, or inaccuracies.

TABLE OF CONTENTS

Introduction 1

Chapter 1 : Black River, White Powder..................................11
    Pablo Emilio Escobar Gaviria...11
    The City Of Eternal Spring 14

Chapter 2 : Smuggler Country..19
    The Marlboro Man 19
    Leaves, Paste, And Powder 25

Chapter 3 : Plata O Plomo 33
    "A Man With A Very Powerful Aura" 33
    Medellin Cartel..38
    A Tale Of Two Cities 44

Chapter 4 : El Presidente Pablo 49
    The Robin Hood Of Antioquia 49
    Death To Kidnappers 54
    Death Of A Minister 59

Chapter 5 : A Man On The Run..65
    Exile 65
    The Extraditables 71

Chapter 6 : Pablo Escobar: International Terrorist.................75
    Black November 75
    The Bloodbath 81

Chapter 7 : The Downfall 95
    The Great Hunt 96
    Los Pepes And The Fall Of Pablo Escobar 102

Conclusion : The Sun Sets Over Medellin 115

References 119

INTRODUCTION

Around 8:30 p.m. on the night of April 30, 1984, the streets of Bogota, Colombia were still packed with bumper-to-bumper traffic. Bogota, the capital city, housed some of the most important government buildings in the nation, and staffers were always coming in and out with security details during all hours. Senators, ministers, congressmen, chairpersons, and their armed escorts often didn't leave work until quite late, particularly when important and time-sensitive government discussions were being tabled. On this night in particular, one especially contentious issue was at hand. The top members of the government had, for some time, been discussing the possibility of allowing the nation's numerous convicted drug offenders to be extradited to the United States of America, the country where the vast majority of their illegal narcotics were destined. One of the fiercest proponents of a new extradition treaty was Minister of Justice Rodrigo Lara Bonilla, one of Colombia's foremost politicians.

Lara Bonilla was certainly an accomplished man. At just 37 years old, he was already a force on the national political scene, but his accomplishments began when he was much younger. As a young man in his early twenties, he was elected Mayor of the town of Neiva in the Huila Department of Colombia, his hometown. Before that, he took up the study of law at Bogota's prestigious Universidad

Externado de Colombia. Then, in 1983, he was chosen to become the Justice Minister in the cabinet of conservative Colombian President Belisario Betancur Cuartas. Betancur had his own goals, of course; his Presidential campaign was largely based on establishing peace with the nation's various insurgent guerrilla groups, including M-19 and the infamous and terroristic FARC. The country had been plagued with political strife for well over a century, and Colombians, especially those living in the vast countryside, were eager to see it come to an end.

Lara Bonilla, however, was head of the Justice Department, and as such, his principal role was that of a crusader against drug trafficking, a criminal enterprise that had long been the bane of Colombia. In this, he was largely successful. He aided in the prosecution of numerous drug traffickers and hoped to use these victories to strengthen his political career. Maybe one day, he could even make a bid for the Presidential office. Either way, the man was ambitious and he had a promising future ahead of him. Lara Bonilla had certainly become a powerful man, but in Colombia in the 1980s, not even the most powerful politician was untouchable, because politics was simply not where the true power resided.

On that April night in 1984, Lara Bonilla was a bit uneasy. During his time as Minister of Justice, he had made more than a few powerful enemies in the country's criminal underworld. Although most of the men who wanted him dead lived in faraway cities in different parts of the country, there was no telling what they could be capable of or how far their wealth and influence extended. The Minister had been receiving death threats almost constantly since he began his crusade against the drug smugglers, and they were credible, too. Countless men had been gunned down since the mid-

1970s for daring to stand up to the power that the drug lords held, and politicians were not excepted. Even police officers had targets on their heads. Armed violence terrorized the city streets in most major cities. Although Colombia was not involved in any foreign conflicts at the time, it's safe to say the country was at war; and, in this war, literally no one was safe.

For Lara Bonilla, the fear of being the next prominent Colombian to be shot dead in the street by hired assassins wasn't enough to drive him out of the country. He did, however, fear for his family. The drug lords were certainly not above kidnapping, torturing, and murdering the loved ones of their enemies, as they had proven time and again, and this was something that the Minister couldn't stomach. Supposedly, he was planning on leaving Colombia around the middle of May, which was less than a month away. As it turned out, this wasn't soon enough. As Lara Bonilla headed home on the last day of April, riding in his luxury Mercedes-Benz, his driver ran into a traffic jam on Bogota's Avenue 127. For Colombian hit men, traffic jams were like an open invitation from God himself. Alongside Bonilla's Mercedes pulled up two men riding a flashy Yamaha motorcycle. This alone would have put Bonilla on edge—motorcycles were prized by gunmen for their maneuverability and ability to weave between cars in traffic. Before his security detail could possibly respond, the man sitting behind the driver of the Yamaha retrieved a M-10 submachine gun he had concealed in his jacket. He took aim at the backseat of the Mercedes where he knew Bonilla would be hiding. He unloaded the clip, and gunfire tore through the windows of the car, hitting Bonilla several times and killing him instantly. Colombia's Minister of Justice, one of the premier cabinet members in the Federal Government, lay dead at the hands of drug peddlers.

Ivan Dario Guisado was the man who pulled the trigger, but he was simply a foot soldier. Responsibility for Lara Bonilla's death was held by none other than Pablo Emilio Escobar Gaviria, unquestioned leader of the notorious Medellin cartel and probably the only man in the country with the power, resources, and audacity to slaughter a member of the Presidential cabinet. He also happened to be the most infamous and feared drug kingpin the world had ever known.

Pablo Escobar had built a veritable empire on the manufacturing and smuggling of a white, powdery substance known by the locals as *cocaina,* or cocaine in English. Not only was this narcotic highly addictive to its users, but it sold for a very high price in countries rich enough to afford such a luxury. Having flooded wealthy American cities like Miami and Los Angeles with the drug for years, Pablo Escobar also became one of the wealthiest men of the 20th century. With this wealth, there was almost nothing he couldn't do, including waging an actual war against the government of Colombia itself. Rodrigo Lara Bonilla was just one of many victims of Pablo's ambition.

For all his wealth, power, and influence, Pablo Escobar had cocaine to thank. Neither Colombia nor the United States were unfamiliar with drugs, but cocaine, a relatively newly developed drug, completely changed the world of narcotics smuggling for both countries. Prior to the introduction of the white powder, marijuana absolutely dominated the drug scene. In its smokable flower form, marijuana was popular among most levels of society in Colombia and America. It was used recreationally and medicinally, and it was in circulation among the Native American communities in Colombia, Peru, Ecuador, Mexico, and elsewhere. It had also been used ceremonially for centuries. Marijuana is not addictive in the physical sense, but it was popular and accessible enough to be a valuable commodity for smugglers. When cocaine was introduced into the market, however, the profit from the sale of marijuana suddenly seemed like chump change.

Unlike marijuana, cocaine is a highly refined product that goes through a lot of chemical processing before it's ready for sale. But, like marijuana, it is also derived from a plant—specifically from variations of the *Erythroxylum coca* species of plant that is native to Colombia, Ecuador, Peru, and other Andean regions. With its characteristic yellow flower petals and red berries, coca leaves were a prized commodity in South America long before European settlers arrived in the New World. Ancient indigenous societies discovered that chewing the coca leaves produced a slight sense of euphoria, as well as sharpened focus and clearer senses. It also helped greatly with dampening the symptoms of altitude sickness, which made it invaluable for communities living in the elevated regions of the Andes mountain range (which stretches along the entire western coast of South America from Colombia in the north to Chile in the south). Some even believe that the great ancient civilization of the Incas used the coca leaf to supercharge the productivity of their people, leading to great feats of architecture and ancient engineering. Unfortunately, when the first chemists discovered that a powerful narcotic could be derived from the leaves of the plant, its long-term effects were found to be more destructive than anything.

From the time cocaine entered the Colombian market, the history of the drug and the country have been intertwined. As early as the late 1970s, Colombia had already become synonymous with cocaine production. A country that just years earlier most Americans couldn't find on a map now evoked images of gang violence and drug wars. The outrageous profits generated from selling to consumers in America were used to purchase police officers, politicians, and the most lavish luxuries the world could offer. The violence that it brought, however, ushered in a new era for Colombian society, as both drug lords and the government slaughtered their perceived enemies with reckless disregard. Colombian cities, especially Medellin, existed in a constant state of terror for over a decade, all for the sake of protecting the smuggling networks that men like Escobar established. It's fair to say that cocaine single-handedly changed the fabric of everyday life in Colombia forever.

For many Americans, it might be difficult to even imagine the kind of power that Pablo Escobar gained from the sale of cocaine alone. Americans are more than familiar with organized crime, as the Italian-American Mafia has been a major influence in most American cities since the late 19th century. However, the Colombian variant of organized crime that came to its full potential in the early 1980s was something completely different.

To the criminal kingpins in Medellin and in Cali, even the most powerful American mobsters like Vito Genovese and Joseph Bonanno probably seemed like amateurs. American gangsters had some degree of political power, and it was relatively easy to buy a senator or two to sway laws in their favor. Escobar, meanwhile dominated the Colombian government with fear. Mafiosos in New

York City could bribe some cops to ignore their crimes, or they might have had a police chief that owed them a favor. On the streets of Medellin, cops either bent their knees to the cartel or faced public execution. And, although American mobsters were responsible for more than a few police slayings in their history, they never had the resources to be able to seriously challenge the United States government in an all-out armed conflict. Pablo Escobar, on the other hand, had a bona fide paramilitary at his disposal, with hit squads that could reach almost anyone at any time, from lowly street criminals to high-level politicians.

Even Escobar's lowest street-level guys were always more well-equipped than the average police officer, and entire police precincts were subjugated by the drug lords. While the Americans were able to eventually dismantle the Mafia crime families in the 80s and 90s using laws and legislation, politicians and law enforcement in Colombia found themselves almost powerless next to the strength of the cartels. The reality is that even the top American mobsters could only dream of having the kind of political power and protection that people like Pablo Escobar enjoyed in Colombia.

Pablo was a man with the entire world in his hands. He was certainly the most powerful man in Colombia, and one of the most influential in the world by the mid-1980s. Known for being generous to Medellin's massive poor population, he was also generally more well-respected than the majority of Colombia's lawmakers and elected officials, at least in the poverty-stricken cities and rural country sides. If a concerned citizen happened to have information relevant to the cartel, they'd be much more likely to run to Pablo with their information rather than the police. And, no matter how badly the government wanted to bring him down, it was the senators and congressmen who were afraid of Pablo, not the other way around. Knowing all of this, it might be easy to assume that he was completely untouchable, that nothing could bring down the great Pablo Escobar. As it turned out, though, Pablo went down much the same way as any petty criminal might. There was nothing ceremonial about it, and it wasn't much of a spectacle either. He didn't get his chance to grandstand before his death or make an audacious display of *machismo* like the fictional coke-dealing character of Tony Montana of *Scarface* fame. No, in the end, Pablo died like the street hustler he started out as: gunned down by the law.

Even though Pablo's death, on paper, was anticlimactic, the lead-up to it was anything but. The sense of power and invulnerability that he had is what eventually convinced Colombia and the world that they needed to stop at nothing to get him. In the United States, the era of the war on drugs had made people like Pablo the very picture of immorality, as he had flooded the country with cocaine for over a decade. In Colombia, his brutal reign and disregard for the lives of the nation's leaders and its people had made him public enemy #1. Could the entire nation simply acquiesce and allow a glorified drug dealer to overcome the government? No. By the early 1990s, both of the countries that Pablo affected most severely were pouring everything they had into the hunt for Medellin's kingpin. Prison wouldn't be enough—Pablo had to die.

The following chapters will explore the life that Pablo created for himself, how it affected the people around him, and how he constructed a drug empire clothed in intrigue and legend that, to this day, has not been rivaled. They will also detail, in due time, how a man with absolutely everything brought about his own downfall, with a country-wide manhunt that was waged both by the law and by his enemies. Finally, these chapters will explore exactly how Pablo changed the world and how both Colombians and Americans changed their relationship with drugs forever.

CHAPTER 1

BLACK RIVER, WHITE POWDER

To understand exactly how Pablo Escobar became the man he was by the mid-1970s, it's important to understand both where and when he came from. Many of the most famous American gangsters grew up in neighborhoods stricken with poverty and spurts of violence, which many have used to explain their criminal past. If their underprivileged upbringing did indeed translate into a successful career in crime, the same is doubly true for Pablo. The kind of poverty he faced in a small Colombian village in the 1940s and 1950s made even the most abjectly miserable American neighborhoods seem like opulent luxury. As we'll see, Pablo's rise to incalculable wealth was anything but predetermined, and his start to life was not exactly auspicious.

Pablo Emilio Escobar Gaviria

On the first day of December 1949, Pablo Escobar was born in a town called Rionegro, which in English translates to "Black River." His mother and father had high hopes for the newest addition to their family, but exactly 44 years and 1 day later, he would be dead at the hands of the Colombian government. Pablo evidently had very high hopes for himself as well, but his measure of success was much different from that of his parents. This was in no small part due to the environment Pablo was born into. Like nearly every Colombian child of his generation, Pablo was thrust into a world where violence seemed to be the only language that people understood. Violence was a way to achieve political power, win arguments, get rid of annoyances, and settle scores. Most importantly, it seemed like virtually the *only* way for someone to get rich in Colombia.

Pablo, who was named after his paternal grandfather Pablo Emilio, was the third child out of seven born to Abel Dari Escobar and Hermila Gaviria. The eldest son of the bunch was Roberto de Jesus Escobar, who served as an early mentor figure and role model to young Pablo, who was born less than three years later. Pablo loved his entire family, but he and Roberto were particularly close, and it was Roberto that would end up helping Pablo found the first incarnation of the Medellin cartel. Both of them, as well as other members of the family, would indeed become ridiculously wealthy people. However, during their early years in Rionegro in the 1940s and early 1950s, things were about as desperate as they could be. Their mother Hermilda worked as a schoolteacher bringing in a modest income, but their father Abel, though he apparently worked several jobs, was a poor laborer for much of his life. Pablo's childhood experiences bred into him a strong hatred for poverty. He hated how little he, his family, and his friends had, and he had a deep resentment for those rich Colombians that lived in the fancy, expensive neighborhoods in the big cities. These rich people seemed to own more than the Escobars could ever dream of. In his youth, he dreamed of escaping poverty and bringing his family along with him, and ensuring that future generations would not have to live through such struggles. These ambitions fomented a strong left-wing ideology in the young, politically-minded Pablo; this social consciousness continued and grew stronger well into his adult years.

Pablo was not nearly the only one in Colombia that wanted to see a change. Unfortunately, for the only adult role models that Pablo had, there was only one way to achieve change: by force. When Pablo was born in 1949, Colombia was in its second year of a brutal civil war that was known by locals as "La Violencia" or "The Violence." The Violence erupted after the assassination of Jorge Elicier Gaitan, a prominent leftist politician and favorite to win the 1949 Colombian election. The conflict raged on until 1958, when Pablo was nine years old. The conflict and violence of the time were almost exclusively political in nature; the key players involved were the Liberal and Conservative Parties, who had been at each other's throats literally since the nation won its independence in the early 19th century. The civil war was fought almost exclusively in the Colombian countryside, so many of those living in the big cities were spared, but this also meant that the rural folk bore the brunt of the horror. War tore across the Colombian plains and mountains, terrorizing villages. Pablo's, of course, was no exception.

When he was just seven years old, guerilla soldiers stormed through Rionegro, abusing, kidnapping, and slaughtering anyone they thought may have been sympathetic to the government. Since there was no use running, Abel and Hermilda tried desperately to hide their several children in their modestly-sized home while they hurried to blockade the doors and windows with makeshift barriers. It was no use. The rebels instead set the Escobar family home ablaze to either kill them or smoke them out. Pablo's life, and the lives of his family, were nearly snuffed out in an instant, but fate intervened. Government forces responded swiftly, riding into the town with guns blazing, driving the guerillas out and chasing them into the mountains. Other soldiers stayed behind to secure the area and lend help to the residents. Pablo's family was rescued from their burning home, and quickly they and the other survivors were escorted to a nearby schoolyard where they could be better protected. As young Pablo was being shepherded to safety, he was paraded past heaps of dead bodies belonging to both the guerillas and their victims. The corpses were shot, dismembered, burned, and mutilated, and Pablo saw all of it, exposing him to some of the worst brutality imaginable at a very young age.

Needless to say, this environment profoundly shaped the man that Pablo became and how he looked at life. Like most of the other children at Pablo's age, he was conditioned to expect little more than a brutal and short life, one that would likely end at the hands of government forces or overzealous rebel forces. Death seemed to be everywhere, to the point that the kids who were born into it became almost numb to it. Perhaps this was simply the way the world worked, they thought. This instilled in Pablo a kind of bravado, a fearlessness toward death that helped propel him to the very peak of the criminal underworld. From a very young age, Pablo knew that he had almost nothing to lose, but the whole world to gain.

The City of Eternal Spring

After the horrors that The Violence had inflicted upon the Escobar family, Hermilda and Abel decided it was time for a change. They couldn't yet uproot the entire family, but Pablo and Roberto were soon sent to live with their grandmother in a small borough on the outskirts of Medellin. Colombia is divided into 'departments,' similar to American states, and Medellin was the capital and largest city of the Antioquia department, which Rionegro is also a part of. Although Medellin was rife with poverty and petty crime, it was still considered safer than the countryside; it was, in fact, shielded from the worst aspects of The Violence. Still, surviving was something of a struggle, and out of necessity, it was here in Medellin that Pablo first began his criminal career. Like many kids who grew up impoverished on the outskirts of Colombia's major cities, Pablo learned to make ends meet by lying, stealing, and conniving. He started off as one of Medellin's countless young pickpockets, bumping into folks on the street on purpose and apologizing before making off with whatever they could grab out of their pant pockets or purses. As Pablo grew older, his scams grew more sophisticated; eventually, he started forging counterfeit high school and college diplomas and selling them to non-graduates looking to apply for jobs they weren't qualified for. His methods of making money also got a bit stranger—he was known to steal tombstones from grave sites and sand off the inscriptions so he could resell them at a discount to the poor families of recently deceased. (And there was no shortage of customers, either.) Eventually, Pablo graduated to grand theft auto, stealing cars with a small gang and reselling them or chopping them for parts.

Nicknamed "The City of Eternal Spring" for its year-round mild climate, Medellin was the second largest city in the entire country, behind only the capital city of Bogota. Traditionally though, it had always been considered a kind of backwater. To the rest of the country, the people there were seen as backwards and anything but refined. They spoke with funny accents and were referred to as *paisa*, which basically meant "country folk." Bogota was where the old money and the landed aristocracy were, whereas Medellin (pronounced by local *paisas* as meh-deh-jeen) and the rest of Antioquia were populated by 'hicks.' By the time Pablo was through, though, this image had changed drastically. Medellin had become a place where seemingly anyone could get wildly wealthy if they were only willing to dabble outside the law and into the lucrative and booming business of drug smuggling that Pablo helped to usher in. But, at the same time, the city was also transformed from a relatively safe urban center to the most dangerous city in the world by far. This, too, was Pablo's doing.

Colombia had been a violent place for a very long time, but as we know, it was almost exclusively political in nature. By the 1970s and especially the early 1980s, though, political violence was largely a thing of the past. Rebel militias were replaced by cartel *sicarios* and hitmen. Colombia's premier source of violence was now the wars among the narcotics kingpins, and political groups were no longer the most powerful groups in the country, especially Antioquia. Colombia never fully rid itself of the plague of political strife, but as we'll see in the following chapters, the country's various insurgent guerilla groups could not hold a candle to the power that the cartels wielded, and Pablo Escobar was at the very top of that heap.

Surprisingly, drugs and drug use were not particularly popular in Medellin before the rise of Pablo, and as far as law enforcement was concerned, it wasn't exactly a top priority to go after drug users or sellers. Marijuana was around in the cities, of course, but in the 50s and 60s, that was mostly in the domain of small-time criminals and recreational users who lived in the mountains and generally grew it themselves. Marijuana was certainly not big business, and more importantly, it was very rarely exported outside the country for profit. Coca, too, was popular in some parts of the country for centuries, but its refined powder form was years away from mass production. (Meanwhile, chewing the leaves was common among the indigenous groups only.)

Medellin's casual relationship with drugs ended harshly with Pablo. When he and Roberto first relocated there, it (along with other big cities) was considered a refuge from the violence that plagued the country. But, by the time Pablo reached middle age, it was these same cities that became the epicenters of a whole new breed of violence, one that the new age of cocaine smuggling had brought to the forefront. The streets of Medellin would soon become warzones, and municipal police forces—most of whom were equipped with nothing but outdated six-shooters—were ill-equipped to deal with what was coming.

CHAPTER 2

SMUGGLER COUNTRY

In hindsight, much of the story of Pablo and Colombia seems predictable. In a country with so much civil unrest and a sophisticated criminal underworld that flourished in chaos, it makes sense that some mastermind could eventually rise to be powerful enough to challenge even the government. The Presidential office in Colombia was far from all-powerful, and with how little a salary public servants earned, bribing them en masse was no difficult task. The geography of the country also helped develop incredibly complex smuggling networks, which propelled the country to the top of the cocaine trade. Situated right between the main coca-producing regions (Peru, Ecuador, and Chile) and the main destination for cocaine exports (North America), Colombia was uniquely positioned to be the middleman in the business. Plus, many of Colombia's top criminals were already seasoned smugglers who had recently started dealing in marijuana. By the early 1970s, Colombia was primed to become a cocaine smuggler's paradise.

The Marlboro Man

For decades, smuggling been a major part of the fabric of Colombian society, and within it, the city of Medellin central. Goods smuggled both into and out of the country would often pass through Medellin, and because so many there lived in poverty, there was a huge market for cheap and counterfeit goods. During the first years of Pablo's time in Medellin, this smuggling didn't include international narcotic sales, though marijuana soon became quite profitable due to its light weight that made shipping cost-effective. Rather, most of the big, old-school smuggling kingpins dealt in consumer goods, especially home electronics. Radios and televisions were especially hot items because they were far too expensive for Medellin's poor population to afford to purchase them legally. American brand names were very popular, and smugglers could bring the contraband items in from places like Panama and sell them for a fraction of what Colombian retailers charged, and still make significant profits. For anyone willing to do some cross-country driving and bribe a few customs officials, it was a good way to make a living.

Televisions and kitchen appliances were good business, but by far, the most lucrative and most frequently smuggled product was cigarettes. In the 1950s and 1960s, Colombians (and *paisas* especially) were obsessed with American cigarettes in particular and were willing to pay good money to get their hands on them. Like marijuana, cigarettes were incredibly light and easy to transport, and pound for pound, they were far more profitable than electronics and other home goods. One truck's worth of televisions would fetch a fair price, but it could easily be doubled or tripled if it were filled with cartons of Pall Malls or Camels. For Colombians, the highly sought-after Marlboro Red cigarette was king. The insatiable clamor for Marlboro cigarettes and the easy profits they guaranteed would play a very important role in Pablo's early life and burgeoning criminal career.

Marlboros were a staple in Medellin's criminal underworld by the time Pablo and Roberto arrived to live with their grandmother in the 1950s. Even after the introduction of cocaine, American cigarettes were very profitable; as late as 1998, contraband Marlboros were considered a major legal problem. *Paisas* preferred illegal American cigarettes so much that it actually drove many local tobacco companies to the verge of bankruptcy. There were hundreds of thousands of dollars up for grabs, and in Medellin, Pablo was steadily honing his criminal skills. As a young man, he plied his trade by boosting cars and flipping them, which proved to be a useful segue into the transportation of illegal goods. It wasn't long before Pablo got involved in the prominent Medellin smuggling rings.

The region of Medellin that Pablo (and eventually his whole family) relocated to was known as Envigado. It was a place rife with crime and poverty, and the streets were prowled by opportunistic muggers who were willing to do anything, even murder, to get by. The deprivation and hardship were not at all new to Pablo, but what was new was the ritzy, studded El Poblado neighborhood nearby that stood in stark contrast to the hopelessness of Envigado. El Poblado, with its gilded nightclubs and luxurious condominium buildings, was where all of Medellin's richest citizens lived. They were the people with connections, and they were the ones that could have anything they wanted while the people around them suffered. Kids like Pablo grew up selling truckloads of illegal cigarettes just to be able to approach the kind of wealth that the people in the neighborhood just north of Envigado had. To Pablo, this disparity was a grave injustice, and witnessing the contrast between the haves and the have-nots firsthand was deeply troubling. His yearning to escape this life became even more intense.

In the late 1960s, as Pablo was approaching his twenties, cocaine in its powder form was first being introduced into the Colombian underworld. However, it was still being sourced and manufactured in very small amounts. Meanwhile, cigarette smugglers were becoming more efficient and Pablo was starting to do smuggling runs with his brother and cousin Gustavo Gaviria, another of Pablo's relatives who was foundational in forging Medellin's cocaine empire. But it was not until about 1974 that the young Escobars and Gavirias really established a foothold among the big players. Pablo's entrance into the world of smuggling was, as we know, not exactly surprising. Actually, it may even have been in his blood. There was a legacy of smuggling in the Escobar-Gaviria clan, and Pablo's maternal grandfather Roberto Gaviria was known to be an accomplished bootlegger. He famously had an uncanny knack for evading the law and dodging capture on several occasions. As we'll see, this was a trait he apparently passed on to Pablo.

Pablo and Gustavo's big break in 1974 came when they were taken under the guiding wing of a man known as Don Alfredo Gomez Lopez. Lopez was an exceedingly wealthy man who made his fortunes selling various discount goods to the people of Antioquia. He was an old-school gangster and smuggler who specialized in highly lucrative contraband tobacco. He had a firm grip on the market and moved so many cartons of cigarettes, especially Marlboro Reds, that he earned the nickname "El Hombre Marlboro" or "The Marlboro Man" in English. Working for Lopez, Pablo and his cohort relatives were provided with both protection and an opportunity to learn from one of the best in the business.

They quickly learned how Lopez ran his business and secured his product, purchasing the coveted Marlboros in trade zones like Panama and Aruba legally, then smuggling them into Colombia and reselling them for a fraction of the local retail price. He also learned valuable lessons about the concept of supply and demand. All across Colombia, entire warehouses were stocked up to the rafters with nothing but packs of Marlboro Reds, and many of these were owned by Lopez. The contraband cigarette market needed to be constantly saturated because it needed to remain affordable, and it didn't hurt that the product was horribly addictive. These same principles applied perfectly to cocaine.

Under the tutelage of Don Lopez, Pablo and Gustavo learned everything about cigarettes and how to smuggle them. When they started out, they were essentially just serving as bodyguards for the kingpin, carrying concealed weapons and escorting him around to protect him from the numerous rival smugglers who would've liked to take him down. It didn't take long for the pair to rise through the ranks of Don Lopez' operation, though. To the pair of young smugglers, loyalty was more important than anything else, and the boss greatly respected it. They quickly gained Don Lopez's trust, and by the end of their time together, they had become two of his most trusted (and feared) enforcers. As it turned out, strong and trustworthy enforcers were exactly what he needed, because as Pablo and Gustavo were coming into their own, the competition between Antioquia's top smugglers was beginning to heat up in a violent way.

Smugglers like Don Lopez and Don Alberto were often at each other's throats over control of the illegal cigarette market, and at some point after Pablo and Gustavo joined up, tensions exploded into all-out war. The infamous conflict became known as the "Marlboro Wars," and every major cigarette trafficker participated in some way. The war was actually a long time coming, and it had everything to do with how high of a demand there was in the cities and how flooded the market had become. As Pablo explained himself, the whole thing began because "Don Alfredo [Lopez] would bring in so many trucks, Don Alberto would bring in other trucks, and Jaime Cordona would bring in some other trucks. The cigarettes would be placed in the market, and because the saturation of product every day was higher, the competition increased, the price would go down, and everyone would lose money. So, the first bullets started flying" (quoted in Micolta, 2012). So, the popularity of their product actually turned out to be detrimental to them, as so many smugglers were trying to break into the market that dealers got caught in a race to the bottom with their prices in order to entice customers.

During the Marlboro Wars, Pablo Escobar served admirably as a wartime lieutenant for Lopez, and both he and Gustavo earned valuable experience in how to deal with competition in the smuggling world. Clearly, sometimes violence and brutality had to be used to assert oneself among their rivals and to eliminate the people who wanted to take their market away. He also learned a lot about the dangers of market saturation and what price deflation could do to a business. This was an experience that Pablo would use to great effect later in his life, but he also couldn't help but wonder how much more profitable the various smuggling gangs could have been if they colluded and worked together rather than starting wars with each other. Perhaps, if the disjointed clans could actually coalesce around a single strong leader, they could build something that no one else could ever challenge. Here, after the violence of the Marlboro Wars, the first kernel of the foundation for the Medellin Cartel formed in Pablo's head. For the time being, he was still working under Don Lopez after the war had wrapped up. Eventually, Pablo and Gustavo were promoted and became key partners in the business.

Leaves, Paste, And Powder

Variations of the modern form of cocaine were first synthesized from the coca leaf in the mid-to-late 1850s, and its potential medical uses were studied intensively in the following years. As a result, many medicinal products containing rudimentary forms of cocaine made their way to market in Europe and the United States in the decades after. The depth of the product's addictive properties was not yet fully understood, especially by consumers, and its use was so widespread that it was even given to children. But it didn't take long for users to discover that the 'medicine' also worked great as a recreational narcotic. In Europe, cocaine was often mixed with alcohol to produce a popular wine drink, and in the United States, a form of cocaine was used as a main ingredient in the first iteration of Coca-Cola. It was becoming a very popular product outside of the medical world, but it had some crippling side effects. Several of the doctors who experimented with cocaine became hopelessly addicted and had their lives destroyed. American religious groups took note of the effect of cocaine and they likened it to alcohol, a product that they had long fought to outlaw in the country. In the early 20th century, when America was going through a kind of religious revival, drugs like cocaine were villainized and eventually made illegal.

For decades, cocaine fell out of the collective American psyche as marijuana was the far more popular drug and took up most of the government's attention. Then, in the 1960s, the United States went through a drastic change in its relationship with drugs. The government still ran intense anti-drug propaganda, but the rise of the "Hippie" movement encouraged an entire generation to begin experimenting with mind-altering and psychoactive substances. Marijuana was by far the most popular, but as the 1960s progressed, more and more powerful drugs started to enter hippie circles around the country. Hallucinogens like psilocybin mushrooms and LSD (known as "acid") became very popular, and toward the tail end of the new drug craze, cocaine was also introduced. It wasn't quite so popular at first, but it was definitely there to stay.

As cocaine began to reemerge in the American market, the powder was still being sourced from South America, but not Colombia. Coca plants were indigenous there, but the smuggling networks didn't have the capability to grow and process them in significant quantities. Instead, it was Chile, a country to the south of Colombia, that was the hub of cocaine trafficking. This was the case in the 1960s and early 1970s, but in 1973, the Chilean government was violently seized by the brutal dictator Augusto Pinochet. At the behest of the anti-drug American government, the new Pinochet regime began brutally persecuting anyone even suspected of drug manufacturing. In very short order, the cocaine industry in Chile was toppled, leaving a vacuum in the smuggling world that was soon to be filled by Pablo Escobar, the young smuggler from Medellin who was still running cigarette shipments. The market gradually shifted to Colombia, a country primed to explode in the smuggling business. There, in Medellin, the cocaine trade was revolutionized.

When Colombian smugglers started to really break into the cocaine market, the new powdery product already threatened to take the entire smuggling industry by storm. Unfortunately, although there were many seasoned Colombian smugglers, the methods of operation at the time were still crude and fairly simple, which capped the amount that they could process through the country. One of the first major cocaine exporters in the country at the time was a woman by the name of Griselda Blanco, who also operated in the city of Medellin. Griselda was a bona fide pioneer in the Colombian cocaine business, and many of the most successful smuggling routes from Peru to the U.S. that Pablo used were actually established by Griselda. It was Griselda who recognized that Miami, New York City, and California were premiere markets for the product.

Griselda started off rather simply, primarily using drug mules to carry the product into America. The mules she used were almost exclusively women who were employed by Griselda. They would strap packages of cocaine to themselves underneath their bras or underwear, and then simply hop on a commercial flight to Miami or New York where the product would be unloaded and distributed. Although the method was modest, it was actually quite ingenious. Women attracted much less attention and were considered less suspicious; plus, concealing the cocaine within their underwear made it far less likely that they would ever be discovered in a search. Only small amounts could be transported at a time, but with powder cocaine being relatively new and hard to come by, Griselda was still making absurd amounts of cash. She went all in on this strategy, and eventually, she used her profits to purchase an entire factory in Medellin that produced women's clothes. Unbeknownst to authorities at the time, Griselda was actually using the factory to mass produce special women's undergarments that had secret compartments built in specifically to conceal packages of cocaine. Before Pablo's rise to drug stardom, Griselda was Medellin's top dog.

Under the reign of Griselda Blanco, Colombian smugglers across the country quickly took note of the profits that could be made from the powder. When Pablo, Roberto, and their cousin Gustavo discovered that they could double, triple, or even quadruple their income from selling cocaine rich *paisas* and to the *gringos* (Spanish slang for Americans), they were floored. Cocaine, they figured, would be just as easy to smuggle as marijuana. It had an even better value-to-weight ratio than the prized Marlboros, and pound for pound, it was more valuable than cigarettes and weed combined. In the mid-1970s, Pablo was still desperately looking to insulate himself from ever returning to a life of poverty, and both he and Gustavo were eager to break into the market before it became flooded. The only problem was that Don Alfredo Lopez, their boss and mentor, did not. Don Lopez knew that there would be inherent risks associated with dealing in cocaine, especially if the product was being funneled into the United States. The *gringos*, he thought, would cause serious trouble. Lopez was a smuggler of the old-school variety, and true to form, he preferred to stick to the old classics: radios, televisions, and smokes. The return was paltry compared to narcotics, but it was much safer; although he was clearly willing to go to war over cigarettes, he was not prepared to face the intense competition and violence that cocaine would soon be bringing to the country. Pablo and Gustavo, who were much younger, were less afraid. They knew getting rich would come with risks, and safety was not worth becoming poor again. By the middle of the 1970s, Pablo was beginning to peddle powder cocaine.

Undeterred by Don Lopez's advice, Pablo Escobar, Gustavo Gaviria, and their crew soon began to break away from the Lopez crew. By 1976, they went off to start their own business in drugs. Pablo and Gustavo had already been operating their drug side business for some time, but that year marked the true breakaway of the Escobar faction. Apparently, there were no hard feelings about the split, and Pablo remained amicable with his mentor for the rest of their lives. Around the same time, though, Pablo was arrested after he was caught trying to boost a car parked on the street. He was sent to La Ladera, a jail in Medellin for criminals serving shorter sentences. It was the first time Pablo faced any real consequences for his crimes, but according to him, it was a good experience. Apparently, all good criminals need to "spend a little time in the school of prison" from time to time (Martinez and Maria, 2017). Pablo wasn't there for very long, but at some point during his stay in La Ladera, he made an important decision. When he emerged as a free man again, he was ready to dedicate himself fully to the art of smuggling cocaine. The only problem was that he was just one of thousands of Colombian criminals trying to seize the opportunity.

In the Colombian landscape, smugglers found a true paradise. The law was already relatively lax toward smugglers before cocaine was introduced, and the methods of detecting incoming and outgoing contraband were not sophisticated enough to stop the criminals who had accumulated decades of experience in smuggling goods of all shapes and sizes. To make matters worse (or, for the smugglers, much better), Colombian police and legal officials weren't exactly dedicated to stopping these criminals. Both cops and judges were also in the market to make some extra cash, as their yearly salaries were usually scarcely enough to get by. If a smuggler did get caught by the cops, being released was usually a simple matter of paying the bribe that the authorities demanded. In fact, the prime motivating factor for cops to catch smugglers was not to clean up Medellin's streets, but rather to extract their payouts. In most cases, the worst that could happen was losing their merchandise. If the smugglers or mules couldn't afford the bribes that the cops demanded, they would have their goods confiscated and would then be sent on their way. To the government, this made more sense than wasting resources to incarcerate the criminals. Even judges in Colombia's high courts were relatively easy to sway with cash. For big cases, the bribe money that a judge could get in exchange for dropping the charges was typically well over a full year's salary. The tight purse strings of the Colombian government allowed the smuggling networks to flourish.

In this environment, Pablo expected to be able to build something truly incredible. The first order of business was establishing a source for the cocaine, and there was no shortage of those. The leaves could be sourced from many countries in South America, but in Peru and Ecuador, the industry was advanced and prepared to meet Medellin's needs. But, processing coca into its final powder form was a multi-step process, and most of the product that Pablo, Gustavo, and Roberto could get from these countries was unfinished, partially refined cocaine paste. It still needed to be processed, heated, dried, and allowed to crystallize into powder before it could hit the market for rich Colombians and Floridians.

To begin their smuggling business, Gustavo was tasked with setting up laboratories and storage facilities in Medellin, where the paste from Peru and Ecuador could be turned into powder in large quantities. From there, it would be packaged and prepared for sale. Gustavo was very successful, and he is largely responsible for turning Medellin into the largest cocaine manufacturing hub in the world.

Pablo and his allies were now ready to assert themselves in the market. Like Griselda, they started out small. Pablo would personally make trips across Colombia to the southern borders with Ecuador and Peru. There, he would purchase the paste, usually just a few kilograms worth at a time, and drive all the way back up to Medellin, the northernmost of Colombia's three major cities. With such small quantities being moved at a time, one could hardly call Pablo Escobar a kingpin, but for the moment, everything seemed to be running smoothly. But it didn't take long for the young gang to hit their first snag. In mid-June of 1976, the same year that Pablo broke away from Don Lopez's clique, the Colombian Department of Administrative Security (DAS) staged a raid on several locations throughout the country to try to hamstring the cocaine barons. In a town called Itagui about 20 minutes outside of the Medellin metropolitan area, DAS agents discovered dozens of pounds of cocaine stuffed into the spare tire of a truck. They determined that Pablo Escobar was the one who owned the truck and the building, and they were determined to throw the book at him. Pablo wasn't too worried at first, but the arresting agents Luis Vasco and Jesus Hernandez proved themselves to be far more principled than Pablo expected. They refused to accept his bribes and hauled him off to prison once again.

This was Pablo's first major run-in with the DAS but it certainly wouldn't be his last. According to what he himself told one of his top hitmen, a man known as Popeye, it was also his first major mistake. Luckily though, this also started Pablo's decade-long streak of good fortune when it came to avoiding legal punishment. Although the DAS agents who arrested him had the moral fortitude to strongly refuse his attempt at buying them off, the judge presiding over Pablo's case in court turned out to be far more 'cooperative.' It's not known for sure how much Pablo's crew coughed up to get the boss free, but it must have been a considerable amount. After spending just a few months in a prison cell, Pablo was once again a free man. He eagerly returned to Medellin, his base of operations, *still* utterly convinced that his true calling was in the drug trade. The outcome of this episode with agents Vasco and Hernandez would have some serious repercussions later on in Pablo's life, as the year 1976 turned out to be a major turning point in his career. For now, though, the issue was laid to rest.

CHAPTER 3

PLATA O PLOMO

After the 1976 Itagui fiasco is when Pablo truly began his ascension to the top tier of drug smuggling royalty. He was ready to commit his life to the trade and was completely undeterred by the possibility of prison or death. As Pablo climbed higher and his success grew, so too did he alter the fabric of society more profoundly. Cities that Pablo's burgeoning empire touched, in both the United States and Colombia, became fundamentally different places as the 1980s approached. Southern Florida, for example, was never quite the same after the introduction of cocaine, and major cities there quickly developed an insatiable demand for more. As the cocaine industry became more efficient and sophisticated to meet the skyrocketing demand, Pablo knew he would have to assert himself as the leader of a cohesive and unified network of top smugglers based out of Medellin. The coalescing of the Medellin cartel was an ominous sign for the future.

"A Man With A Very Powerful Aura"

Anyone who knew Pablo as a person wouldn't have been surprised to see him rise above his peers and take on the premiere leadership position of the new Medellin organization. Even when he was a child in Rionegro, Pablo had a very strong personality, and he began displaying strong leadership qualities when he was a young man growing up in Envigado. He cared deeply for his friends and family and showed an eagerness to do anything he could for them. He showed immense loyalty to the people close to him, and in turn, he found it quite easy to attract loyal followers, even in his youth. Even after he began to find success in the world of crime, he never changed who he was. He remained true to his personality and was always genuine Pablo, for better or worse. Perhaps most importantly, he was as humble as ever despite his increasing fortune, and he was never arrogant toward the people he respected.

Pablo had immense natural charisma that made him a generally very likable young man. When he and his friends started their very first gang as street youths, he quickly amassed a select group of followers that would listen to his every word. Many of them continued to follow Pablo into the cocaine revolution and stuck by him to the very end. As Pablo was making a name for himself by stealing cars and smuggling contraband into the city, he and his personal gang commonly referred to as *Los Pablos* also began to form a close relationship with the local Medellin police department as well as the chief of police. Having the local cops on their payroll was a huge benefit—it got to the point that police would sometimes give Pablo a heads up if certain cars were reported stolen and conveniently make themselves scarce when the gang wanted to hit a certain lot. Pablo's police and legal connections only grew stronger in the following years, and they helped to secure his new, growing status position in the city. Pablo was no longer an impoverished little boy from the periphery of Antioquia; he was now an up-and-coming Medellin superstar.

Through the 1970s, Pablo continued to grow his base of loyalists and criminal cohorts. As one of his friends explained, "he was like a God, a man with a very powerful aura" (Attwood, 2016). People around him couldn't always explain it, but they were magnetized to Pablo. Aside from just being charismatic, Pablo was also clearly destined to be a businessman. Since he was young, he was constantly working on new ways to make a buck. As a boy, he owned and operated his own bike repair service in Envigado, which would also rent out some bikes for the right price. Business was always good, and once he had saved up enough cash, he bought himself a little Lambretta that he used to dart around the streets of Medellin robbing people blind. It was a crude way to make money, but as he entered adulthood, both his crimes and his methods of conduct became much more refined. Pablo's business philosophy was summed up in three words: *plata o plomo*. In English, this translates to "silver or lead," basically implying that nearly every problem could be solved with money, and those that couldn't, had to be solved with violence. It also served as a subtle warning to any cops or politicians who might try to step up to Pablo. If someone is causing you trouble, bribe them (silver). If that doesn't fix the problem, a hail of machine-gun fire (lead) certainly will.

In 1977, an opportunity to demonstrate what Pablo really meant by *plata o plomo* presented itself. It was just months after Pablo's "cocaine in the spare tire" case was thrown out and after his brief stint in prison. The DAS agents Luis Vasco and Jesus Hernandez who had refused Pablo's bribe and arrested him were furious when he walked free. Eventually, they determined that they would have to take justice into their own hands to do what the judge was unwilling to do. They began looking for Pablo and his close associates, tracking them and noting their routines. One night, an opportunity presented itself. The pair forcefully abducted Pablo and his cousin Gustavo at gunpoint, stuffed them into a car, and drove them both out to a small hill somewhere outside the city limits. They made it clear: Their intention was not to give Pablo another shot in court. They were going to execute them and bury them both under that hill. Pablo always seemed to be able to stay calm under pressure, and as he was forced to his knees with a gun to his skull, he still managed to keep a cool head despite being furious on the inside. Rather than give in to the fear and anger, Pablo respectfully assured them that they were making a mistake. If they would just let him live, he would make them far richer than the judge who let him walk in the first place. He promised a massive payoff. After a heated back and forth, between the agents their prisoners, Vasco gave in. He wasn't fully convinced though. He demanded that Pablo show him where he had the money. They left quickly, and Hernandez stayed back to hold Gustavo prisoner until the cash was confirmed.

By the end of the night, the DAS agents had their cash prize in hand. It's unknown exactly how much they extorted from Pablo, but it was enough to convince the previously implacable Vasco and Hernandez to let the two smugglers live. Pablo and Gustavo were certainly relieved that they left without a bullet in their heads, and Gustavo probably thought that the matter was all wrapped up nicely. For Pablo, though, it was anything but settled. The agents eventually accepted his bribe, yes, but they had sealed their fate the moment they refused him the first time back in 1976. And, when they decided to take violent action against Pablo, they threw forgiveness out the window. Pablo was free again after another close call, but he would never let this go. The disrespect had to be answered for, and Pablo swore that he would never allow himself to be caught that vulnerable ever again.

As soon as Pablo saw Vasco and Hernandez's faces again, he knew what had to be done. Gustavo was shocked when Pablo told him his plan. Could they really do it? Would they actually go so far as to execute two federal agents? Whatever doubts Gustavo had, they didn't matter. Pablo made up his mind, and when Pablo made up his mind, it had to be done. Pablo knew that men like Vasco couldn't be trusted to cooperate. If they continued to live, they would be shaking Pablo and his guys down at every opportunity for years. Besides that, Pablo's ego was bruised, and he needed to correct it. He didn't have to wait long for revenge. One day, in March of 1977, one of Pablo's street guys got a tip that the two DAS agents were spotted having a night out, drinking at a local pub. Pablo reacted quickly. He and Gustavo headed out in their direction and soon spotted them climbing into a car. Gustavo, who was driving, pulled up alongside their car, and Pablo unloaded an entire clip into the vehicle, killing agents Vasco and Hernandez.

The message was sent loud and clear: Pablo Escobar is not one to be taken lightly. Once again, it seemed like the fiasco with the DAS agents was finally over, but it wasn't so simple. This event and others like it would come back to haunt Pablo in a serious way over the next several years. The street execution of two federal agents was not going to be ignored by the government, and it didn't take much to figure out that Pablo was a prime suspect. Still, over the years, his insults and attacks against the government and its agents only increased, and he became more brazen and much more aggressive. There were men who, in the late 1970s, began dedicating their lives to making sure Pablo Escobar met consequences for his streak of terror, but that was a problem for another day. For now, Pablo had police to bribe, judges to buy, drugs to sell, and rivals to slaughter.

Medellin Cartel

In the years leading up to the 1980s, Pablo continued to operate his international drug smuggling business and, even before he reached his peak, he was profiting massively. Even in the early years of the 1970s when Pablo was in his early 20s and wasn't fully independent, he had already amassed a fortune. But, as dominant as he became in the market, he wasn't the only one with the brains to profit off the cocaine trade, and he definitely wasn't the first. Griselda held the spot of Medellin's top smuggler before him, and her success eventually earned her the title of "godmother" of cocaine. She made immense contributions toward Medellin's drug culture, and her smuggling routes that stretched from the Peruvian Andes in the south to the New York City and Canada in the north were examples that younger smugglers looked up to. What's most important for this story, though, is that Griselda also served as a kind of lightning rod, diverting legal attention away from the other up-and-coming smugglers. She was the first Colombian cocaine smuggler that caught the attention of the American government and law enforcement, and they went to great efforts pursuing her endlessly for years, laying responsibility for Miami's drug crisis at her feet.

While American officials suspected Griselda of being the worst offender out of Colombia's cocaine rings, a far more imposing figure was lurking in her shadow. Pablo Escobar was still operating under the radar and he was still relatively unknown to American law enforcement agencies. He wasn't the only one who benefited from Griselda's notoriety in southern Florida and elsewhere.

Among the other rising stars, there were four major traffickers. First, there was Jorge Luis Ochoa Vasquez of the Ochoa clan. About one year Pablo's junior, Jorge and his brothers Fabio and Juan were Medellin natives and had strong connections in the city. Jorge's father Fabio presided as head of a large drug smuggling family. Jorge, a characteristically large man, earned the nickname "El Gordo," or "the fat one." Next, there was Carlos Lehder Rivas, a Colombian-German man who had very strong connections in the United States and had some of the best contacts in the drug smuggling world. The eldest of this bunch, aside from the Ochoa patriarch, was Jose Gonzalo Rodriguez Gacha, also known as "The Mexican," reportedly due to his obsessive appreciation for Mexican culture, literature, and music. Gacha was a former jewel smuggler and had formed a friendship with Pablo Escobar at some point, which prompted him to enter the drug trade, to great success. He found an incredible fortune as a drug baron and, despite the brutal conclusion to his story, was one of Colombia's most powerful figures. He was a relative newcomer to Medellin, having relocated there in 1976, but he enmeshed himself with the underworld there in no time at all. But the last and by far the most powerful and notorious of these smugglers was Pablo, the man who would soon come to be known as "El Patron."

When they were all still in the process of making a name for themselves, Pablo, Ochoa, Gacha, and Lehder were all still operating relatively independently. Lehder was especially distant from the epicenter of this drug revolution, as he was operating almost exclusively in the United States. Around Medellin, though, Pablo and Jorge Ochoa were the kings. On the streets, Pablo's guys were colloquially known as "Los Pablos," while Jorge's group was referred to as "El Clan Ochoa." In English, they were popularly known as "the Ochoa Family," reminiscent of the Italian-American Mafia. Like Pablo, the Ochoa brothers had grown up with a deep resentment toward poverty. Jorge had watched members of his family work themselves nearly to death for years, just to be able to put food on their table each night. He grew up having to watch the tragedy of his mother and sisters endure tedious and brutal working lives, and as he grew older, he decided he would do anything to save them from a life of hardship. The Ochoa family actually had a history in the underground smuggling world, and Jorge was well aware of it. He knew that there was very good money to be earned in that trade. It at least offered more promising prospects than toiling away at a dead-end laborer job. It didn't take very long for Jorge and his brothers to start dabbling in international narcotics smuggling.

Although Lehder, Gacha, Ochoa, and Escobar had separate organizations, they were actually surprisingly cooperative, even in the early years. Pablo and the Ochoa brothers, who had known each other since childhood, were especially close. Although the infamous Medellin Cartel was not yet fully formed, the interconnectedness of these Colombian smugglers was its foundation. Pablo had good reason to ensure that all the top kingpins maintained good relations. Years ago, during the Marlboro Wars, Pablo learned exactly how dangerous and destructive competition could be. The unwillingness of the cigarette barons to work together toward a common goal seriously hindered all of their profits. Much more success could be found, according to Pablo, by coming together as a united front against those wishing to stop them (in particular, the

Colombian government and law enforcement). In his eyes, they were simply stronger together.

Given Pablo's natural charisma, he found it easy to convince the likes of Jorge Ochoa and Jose Gacha to pool resources, share information, and generally avoid confrontation. But the real catalyst for the formation of the Medellin Cartel was a common desire to break deeper into the coveted American market, the one that promised the greatest profits due to its legions of wealthy citizens with disposable income. In the late 1970s, both Los Pablos and the Ochoa Family were desperate to secure a strong foothold in the U.S. outside of their restricted markets in southern Florida. There was big money to be won, but the problem was that neither Pablo nor Ochoa had the experience in America necessary to really break out. Pablo, for one, had never stepped foot in the country. Jorge Ochoa had, but on his only trip there, he was nearly captured by American authorities; as a result, he was a little gun-shy about the idea of taking charge there. Unlike Griselda, Pablo and the Ochoas simply didn't have the connections they needed to be able to push the amounts of cocaine they wanted. As it turned out, the solution to this problem was Carlos Lehder.

Carlos Lehder Rivas was a native-born Colombian but he had been living in the United States since he was just 15 years old, when his mother divorced his Nazi-sympathizing German father and left the country. In America, Lehder eventually became a smuggler. Like Pablo, his first serious criminal business was auto theft. He would secure vehicles in the U.S. and traffic them back to his native Colombia for resale. Afterward, Lehder got into smuggling marijuana which, at the time, was easier to transport in large amounts than cocaine. In the early and mid-1970s, though, most of his weed was being transported between the United States and Canada, so his path did not directly intersect with that of Pablo's. That is, before Lehder was sent to prison in 1974.

There, in Connecticut's Danbury prison, Lehder met George Jung, an American about seven years Lehder's senior who was also serving time for a similar marijuana-related conviction. Obviously, the pair had a lot in common, and they bonded over their shared smuggling experience. Lehder had connections that intrigued Jung, and they started to consider what their options would be when they were released from prison. Perhaps they too would be stronger together. They discussed how they could help the other grow their business, but Lehder had something besides weed in mind when he asked him a fateful question: "What do you know about cocaine?" Lehder knew that there were going to be huge profits once cocaine really made its comeback from its peak in popularity during the 19th century, and Jung was not one to scoff at new opportunities. They wanted to build a sophisticated smuggling network within the United States and Canada, and they agreed to partner with each other once they were free men. There were some unanswered questions, though: Where would they get the cocaine? Who could supply the vast amounts of powder they wanted to move? Lehder knew there was only one man suited for the job—Pablo Escobar Gaviria.

On a personal level, Lehder was quite an awful human being. Many times, Jung was seriously disturbed by his behavior, which would later become a problem for all of his future partners. Lehder had, on one occasion, forced his own mother to traffic cocaine for him, which is what made Jung realize that he was unstable and genuinely dangerous. Most of his eccentricity and behavioral problems were likely due to the fact that, unlike Pablo, Lehder started to get high off his own product. He developed a dangerous relationship with cocaine that eventually made him erratic, neurotic, and constantly nervous. In contrast, Pablo knew the dangers associated with cocaine and, according to all accounts, he steered clear of the powder his entire life, despite possessing a greater amount of it than probably anyone else on earth. Pablo did enjoy smoking marijuana though and apparently indulged in this habit daily. In contrast to the depths of cocaine addiction, it never impacted his duties or responsibilities. Lehder, on the other hand, eventually fell deeper and deeper into his dependency, and by the time his career came to an end, he had turned into an unpredictable, paranoid mess of a person.

Despite Lehder's personal shortcomings, his talent couldn't be denied, and his experience with the American markets had substantial value. Together he and Jung built a solid foundation, but they were unable to fully break into the cocaine craze because they didn't have extensive connections with the source of the coca (which included Peru, Bolivia, and Colombia). Meanwhile, Pablo and the Ochoas couldn't fully dominate the American market because they didn't have experience in the country nor did they have access to all of their smuggling networks. Griselda Blanco proved unwilling to cooperate with anyone or share her resources, so she was not a prime candidate for partnership. Lehder and Jung, however, were perfect. They had opposite problems, and joining forces would bring greater profits to everyone involved. Pablo could easily source the coca paste from Bolivia or Peru, and in Medellin, which he and the Ochoas had turned into a massive cocaine manufactory, they could process it into powder. From there, Lehder and Jung could handle distribution throughout American cities. Lehder himself was actually a trained pilot and didn't mind being in the thick of things, so he would become invaluable for using air transport, something that revolutionized cocaine smuggling. Jose Gacha also created highly sophisticated networks over land through Mexico. Gacha's routes were incredibly valuable for breaking into the California and Texas markets. This early cooperation, which still had not fully formed by 1976, laid strong foundations for what would become the Medellin Cartel.

A Tale of Two Cities

After Lehder was released from Danbury prison, he was promptly deported back to his native Colombia as his mother had brought him there illegally and his immigration status was in question. This, however, was a great benefit. He needed to be back in Colombia anyway to set up his new business, and he had told Jung that, when the time came and everything was in place, he would send a signal for him. Lehder hooked up with Pablo Escobar and explained his intent to smuggle massive amounts of cocaine into the U.S., and Pablo took a liking to him rather quickly. He was impressed with the plan, and he knew this was a good opportunity to get business booming stateside. Pablo agreed to supply the cocaine, and before long, Lehder was transporting unprecedented quantities out of Colombia, with Jung handling distribution in America. With this new alliance, the Medellin drug barons were becoming even more obscenely wealthy than they were with their small shipments. Unfortunately, their partnership also marked the beginning of a new, dark era for both Colombia and America, as the flood of cocaine was creating massive substance abuse problems, and the wealth that was being generated was ramping up competition that had to be brutally repressed. The cities of Medellin and Miami, which became the epicenter for the cocaine market, were becoming warzones, and their stories demonstrate how Pablo's cocaine fundamentally impacted the cities it touched.

As we know, Medellin was not a city unfamiliar with violence even before cocaine took it by storm. It was undoubtedly dangerous, as was the entire Colombian countryside, but the effects of the drug trade were worse than anyone could have imagined. Before long, bodies lined the streets of Medellin, with hit squads roaming around gunning down enemies and rivals on their bosses' orders. Meanwhile, local law enforcement was utterly unprepared to deal with the violence. Medellin's police force was understaffed and underequipped, while the narcotics *sicarios* (hitmen) could afford the best automatic weapons and equipment. Carnage reigned, while men like Pablo, Gacha, and the Ochoas were becoming rich beyond their wildest dreams. In 1978, while the streets of Medellin were becoming sites of brutal attacks and drive-by assassinations, Pablo was able to purchase an absolutely massive 20-square-kilometer estate property in Puerto Triunfo, about 100 miles outside Medellin. The property was known as Hacienda Napoles, and it served as both Pablo Escobar's home and personal playground, equipped with its own exotic zoo (which introduced the hippopotamus into Colombia) and bullfighting ring. Mounted above the property's grand entrance was a replica of the first plane Pablo ever used to fly shipments of cocaine into America.

By the 1980s, Medellin had officially become the most dangerous city in the entire world. For the citizens of the city, however, it had already felt that way for many years. Drug money completely changed the city's landscape. All of the old money families were pushed out, and the industry leaders were no longer Medellin's wealthiest citizens. Instead, they were replaced by drug lords. These coke peddlers eventually bought up all of the city's major industries, both in order to launder their drug money and to generate side income, as well as to increase their power and influence over local politicians. Even outside of the industries, many of the most profitable businesses were tainted by cocaine. Medellin's nightclubs, for example, were invariably owned and operated by local drug lords. The homicide rate was reaching new records every year, and motorcycle drive-bys took the city by storm. Pioneered by Griselda Blanco and perfected by Pablo Escobar, the motorcycle drive-by was a hit-and-run tactic that featured a quick getaway. It was a preferred style of eliminating 'problems' throughout the city. This method was eventually imported into Miami by the cartel.

Cocaine had an impact on most major American cities, but none more so than Miami. It used to be known as a popular retirement destination where old folks from New York and Chicago who were tired of the weather would go to spend their last years. It was a kind of paradise on earth, and many of its beautiful seaside communities were populated almost entirely by senior citizens from up north. In the late 1970s, all of this changed, in large part due to people like Griselda and Pablo. In 1977, Los Pablos finally began using cargo planes to fly their shipments into America, and Florida was the prime destination. The use of planes to ship mass amounts of coke at a time marked a new era for Miami, which was soon transformed from an idyllic utopia into one of the bloodiest cities in America. Rival drug gangs fighting over the Miami market routinely fought in the streets and mid-traffic shootouts were becoming an almost daily occurrence. Spotting a motorcycle in a traffic jam was enough to put the average Miamian on edge. When Cuban smugglers entered the market, they began having wars with the Colombian factions, leading to mass casualties and collateral damage. Like in Medellin, local Miami cops were outfitted with nothing but old six-shooters, yet they were expected to curb the tide of gangsters equipped with the latest Israeli submachine guns. Miami was turning into a playground for drug dealers.

Miami experienced a *major* spike in its murder rate, and the city was eventually named the murder capital of the United States. Pablo had brought so much unexpected carnage that the city had to resort to renting out refrigerated food trucks to store the bodies of dead drug dealers because the morgues were literally too full to take them. The saddest part was that there appeared to be no end in sight. The Colombian and Cuban traffickers were not leaving any time soon, as cocaine was just too profitable there. In Medellin, a kilogram of cocaine might sell for around $8,000 or $9,000, whereas the exact same kilogram could fetch nearly $45,000 in Miami (Gugliotta, 2011). Even with increased government attention, the cash was worth the risk, and Miami's descent into drug-fueled massacres was a small price to pay.

The fates of Medellin and Miami were irrevocably entwined, and they had both turned into centers of murder at the hands of cocaine gunmen looking to snuff out competition. But, as late as 1982, American officials were still largely unaware of the role that Pablo Escobar was playing in all of it, as high-profile and infamous events like the Dadeland Shopping Mall Massacre had cast all attention on Griselda. Pablo would not be able to enjoy his lack of notoriety for much longer, though.

CHAPTER 4

EL PRESIDENTE PABLO

Since Pablo was a young man, he had political aspirations. His left-wing political leanings derived from his experience of poverty in his youth, and these dreams persisted into adulthood. Aside from an insatiable desire to become wealthy, he was also a man who genuinely thought he could make a difference in the world, or at least in his native land. As we'll see, his political instincts were reflected in his leadership of the nascent Medellin cartel, and he was able to foster a favorable public image of himself as a champion of the underclass. In the 1980s, he attempted to ingrain himself into Colombia's political fabric, and he did reap the benefits. However, there was one important drawback: It put the name "Pablo Escobar" on the radar of every important lawmaker in Colombia and, more importantly, America.

The Robin Hood of Antioquia

As Pablo Escobar grew his power into the late 1970s and early 1980s, one thing that became shockingly obvious was that the people of Medellin trusted him more than they trusted their own government. His charity toward the city's most underprivileged earned him a public image as a friend of the poor, one who looked out for those that the government ignored and who helped them whenever he could. He also found it easy to maintain his friendships because he always generously rewarded loyalty, a quality he treasured above all else. He was notoriously slow to anger with his friends, but it was also true that he was even slower to forgive. In his mind, betrayal or treason was always grounds for death. Because of this, only the most foolish would cross him. He was a great friend to have, but a terrible enemy.

While it may be difficult to imagine a drug dealer having such a pristine public persona, it was actually quite easy for Pablo. He discovered very early on that murder was a cheap and highly effective means of maintaining his public relations. Since he was young, he was obsessed with the glamorized gangster lifestyle that he saw in American movies growing up. He loved *The Godfather* and he idealized the portrayals of infamous gangsters like John Dillinger and Al Capone. He longed to be like them, and when he was an adult, he imitated their aggressiveness to a tee. If there was someone talking bad about him or his family around Medellin, they were dead. A pesky cop that's been trying to expose his brutal crimes? He was dead too. A rival that has been making noise about taking him down? That was a major offense, and immediate death would actually be the merciful consequence. For Pablo, it was all a very simple equation. He considered anyone that didn't support him to be an enemy, and his enemies were dropping like flies. He tolerated no dissent within his city, and the only ones that were safe were those who refused to cross him. Murdering so many of his enemies meant that most of the people left were friends, but as we'll see later in Pablo's story, this also made him a *lot* of future enemies.

The families and loved ones of the countless people that Pablo slayed were many, and they weren't quick to forget.

With Pablo making enough money to have just about anyone he wanted killed at any time, his ego grew. His ability to use fear to persuade cops into ignoring his myriad crimes inflated his ego further, but outwardly, he appeared to be the same Pablo he had always been. He didn't become pretentious and, despite taking on the mannerisms of a Hollywood Teflon Don, he didn't act like he was superior to anyone else, particularly the poor. Looking at Pablo, you wouldn't even know that he was the richest man in Colombia. Aside from his massive home at Hacienda Napoles, Pablo never flaunted his cash or his status. In nearly every picture of Pablo, he still wears the same old polo shirts and blue jeans that he wore before he was a billionaire. His style of dress also served a tactical purpose though—on the streets of Medellin, he blended in amongst the masses and any potential hitmen hired by his enemies would be hard-pressed to pick him out of a crowd.

Pablo wasn't just humble with his money. He was also unusually generous. He obviously never stole from the poor and he never exploited those who lived as he used to live in Rionegro. In fact, he was a generous benefactor to the thousands dwelling in Medellin's slums. He fully funded the construction of hospitals and clinics in the city where the poor could receive medical attention. He constructed housing zones in the city and offered the properties to the poor for free or almost free. These were actual homes, significant upgrades over the makeshift shacks crafted from corrugated iron and siding that many of them were used to. He built schools, funded social programs, and even donated money and equipment to local soccer teams. The richer and more successful he became, the more public works and charity programs he funded. If he did anyone wrong, his victims were never those who had life the hardest. Because of this, Pablo was often compared to the fictional Robin Hood, a character who famously stole from the rich and gave to the poor as an act of social justice. Pablo was the Robin Hood of Antioquia.

Even before Pablo was monumentally rich, he had taken on a kind of Robin Hood-esque profile. The most intriguing example of this from his earlier years was the case of the kidnapping and murder of Diego Echavarria Misas. Echavarria was a powerful local business mogul that made his fortune operating successful textile mills. He had for years tried desperately to cultivate an image for himself as a benevolent philanthropist, a saint and a savior of the masses. Underneath the surface, however, Echavarria was only able to maintain profitability at at his mills by brutally exploiting the desperately poor people that he employed there. But he also endowed local schools and made sure his name and face were plastered everywhere. He spread enough money around to get people to love him, and to a degree, it worked. The way Echavarria was treated bordered on hero worship. Children in schools were taught about his good deeds as though the man were Christ himself. In Medellin's business class, he was a very well-respected man.

Like Pablo, he wanted to be seen as a friend of the poor, but unlike Pablo, he was comfortable accomplishing that on the backs of the peasants. His workers were basically indentured servants, who worked ungodly hours and earned just barely enough to keep themselves alive. His rabid desire to expand his property ended up forcing hundreds, possibly thousands of peasants off lands that their families had worked on for generations. Many of the peasants were murdered if they refused, and those that were displaced were forced into Medellin's various slums, clogging and overcrowding the streets. Pablo had never liked Echavarria very much, and it's not known whether Echavarria owed him money or vice versa, or if Echavarria had simply worn out Pablo's patience. What's clear is that, in 1971, he had gone missing. Kidnapped, as it turned out. Police searched Medellin door to door for weeks on end, and just over a month later, his body was found. He had been tortured and then beaten to death. It wasn't known at the time exactly who killed Echavarria, but Pablo was widely believed to have played a role in the decision to both abduct and murder him.

There was a significant public outcry in the wake of his death, and many people were certainly moved by his passing. Even one of Pablo's hitmen, a man known as Popeye, recalled Echavarria fondly when Pablo revealed to him later in life that he was in fact responsible (Legarda Martinez, 2017). But, for as many people who mourned him, there were as many who celebrated his death. Medellin's poor who believed Pablo was responsible thanked him for his service. According to Attwood (2016), many in the slums took to calling him *El Doctor Escobar* out of respect for the man who cured their ills. After his death, his family continued to rehabilitate his image by highlighting his charitable contributions and obscuring the history of his exploitative factories and textile mills. But it didn't matter how the businessman was remembered after his death. Over the course of the next few years, it was Pablo who would become the object of admiration from Medellin's thousands of poor citizens. Combined with his generous charitable works in the slums through the late 1970s, Pablo had created a kind of cult of personality around himself that he would try to fully exploit in the early 1980s.

Death To Kidnappers

The early iteration of the Medellin cartel that formed in 1976 had become much stronger and much more cohesive by 1980, and it's popularly believed that its true inauguration was in 1981. In April of that year, there was a meeting that featured most of the top cocaine kingpins in Colombia. This meeting was held at the Ochoa family estate known as the Hacienda Veracruz. The meeting, which came to be known as the Ochoa Summit, had a very clear agenda. They met to discuss the future of the cocaine business and to plan for expansion over the coming years. Pablo could not be in attendance, but Los Pablos were represented by one of Escobar's top enforcers, a man named Pablo Correa Arroyave, who also happened to be the brother-in-law of Jorge Ochoa. Correa Arroyave was a trusted member of the crew and was actually one of its original founders. In fact, contrary to the popular belief that Pablo Escobar was the crews only namesake, "Los Pablos" referred to Escobar, Pablo Correa Arroyave, and the third cofounder, Pablo Correa Ramos (U.S. Government Printing Office, 1989).

All the representatives were greeted with the finest amenities that money could buy. The opulence of Hacienda Veracruz was just another testament to how absurdly rich the top dogs in the industry had become. And the future was looking even brighter. The main reason that the Ochoa Summit was called in the first place was that Carlos Lehder's lucrative and pioneering transportation routes and networks could no longer handle the volume that the American market was now demanding. According to their own estimates and the estimates of their lawyers and accountants, there were millions, maybe hundreds of millions, going unearned because the cartel couldn't move as much product as Californians and Floridians and New Yorkers were willing to buy. Together, the representatives for Pablo, Ochoa, Lehder, Gacha, and others established goals for future development that would make them all far more successful, but that required new routes. Additional air routes were created, and Gacha's overland network through Mexico was fine-tuned to be able to push more into southern California and Texas, as well as the surrounding markets. The Ochoa Summit was a very strong sign that the various smuggling groups were still working closely together, and to great effect. It also went far in creating a sense of solidarity between their leaders. And, although Jorge Ochoa was the official host of this meeting, there was no question that Pablo Escobar was going to continue to serve as the alpha wolf in the pack of hungry coke peddlers.

The meeting was a key milestone in the solidification of the Medellin Cartel as one unit, but it was only the beginning. The coming months saw a far greater degree of cooperation among the key men. Los Pablos dominated the sourcing of the coca paste that was refined into cocaine, as Pablo himself had key connections in Peru and Bolivia. Most of the manufacturing of the powder also took place in his Medellin factories. Ochoa and Gacha established new and diverse trafficking routes into the southern American states. Carlos Lehder, who was once the main transporter of the merchandise, was now most valuable for his connections in America, particularly in the north of the country (though, in actuality, these connections were mostly secured by the American George Jung).

There was one key figure left out of this new equation, and that was the "godmother" Griselda Blanco. By the time the Medellin Cartel fully came into being, Griselda was being forced to operate largely on the sidelines. This was because of two reasons. First, Griselda was notoriously brutal, even by Pablo's standards. She was also reckless. Her role in the 1979 Dadeland Mall Massacre had immortalized her as a feared and vicious drug lord but also stained her reputation among the other drug barons. High profile shootouts in the U.S., especially those involving the loss of several innocent American lives, drew a lot of heat to the cocaine smugglers, and the attention of the U.S. government was absolutely the last thing they needed. Second, Griselda was simply uncooperative—she refused to take a backseat to anyone and certainly didn't want to share in the profits with any of the other cartel leaders. But this fierce independence aided in her downfall. While the Medellin Cartel reached new heights, Griselda was on the downturn. It was Pablo's time now.

More important than the Ochoa Summit was the formation of a group known popularly as MAS. It stood for Muerte a Secuestradores, or in English, "Death to Kidnappers." MAS was essentially a paramilitary group that was supported and funded by the cartel. Its ranks were staffed with cartel hitmen and soldiers, and its formation was a landmark in the cartel's history. For many years, kidnapping had been a major problem in Colombian society. For opportunistic criminals, it was seen as an easy and reliable way to get a quick payday. The richer the better, and the family and friends of the kidnapped were always willing to pay top dollar to see their loved ones alive and well again. The plague of kidnappings touched every stratum of Colombian society, and even the drug lords weren't immune to it. It was no secret how much men like Pablo were earning, which made them targets for the more brazen of

Colombia's abductors. It was dangerous, but they were tempting targets. Carlos Lehder himself narrowly avoided being kidnapped, and shortly after that, Jorge Ochoa's sister Marta was successfully kidnapped in November 1981. After Marta Ochoa was taken, the top drug lords called yet another meeting, at which Pablo and Jorge were the main leaders. Their goals included outlining a plan to retrieve Marta alive and well and also to lay the foundations for preventing something like this from ever happening again.

The solution they came up with was to form MAS, a group that would actively and aggressively pursue kidnappers and swiftly put to death anyone found guilty. The group was heavily armed and well-equipped, and they were soon to hit the streets in not just Medellin but several of Colombia's large cities. As it turned out, Marta was kidnapped by a group called M-19, one of Colombia's various guerrilla insurgency armies. They were fighting in opposition to the Colombian government and were always looking for sources of funding, unafraid to resort to criminal schemes to do it. In this case, they were attempting to extort the Ochoa family for millions of dollars. At the meeting that founded MAS, Jorge announced that he would refuse to pay a single peso of what M-19 was demanding, and although sources differ, it appears that the Ochoas did in fact pay at least a portion of the ransom to ensure Marta's safety. Most importantly, MAS was not founded solely to protect the trafficking families—it was for the benefit of all Colombians affected by kidnapping. Pablo quickly established himself as the primary representative of MAS, and under his guidance, it actually became quite a popular group among the masses. MAS did much to convince them that perhaps the cartel was not as bad as they had heard.

The cartel decided to announce MAS in a grand fashion. They flew an airplane over a soccer match that was taking place in Cali, Colombia's third largest city which had its own competing cartel that was beginning to form. The plane dropped hundreds of leaflets over the players and spectators, bearing a message that was drafted and approved by drug traffickers from all across the country. It was a stern warning to all potential offenders: Kidnapping would no longer be tolerated within Colombia's borders, and these crimes would be met with swift execution. It called for cooperation from Colombia's decent citizens, and served as a declaration for the *real* outlawing of kidnapping. If Colombia's government was too incompetent to do anything about this plague, then the cartels were willing to take matters into their own hands.

Cali was chosen as the city to announce MAS rather than Medellin for a specific purpose. The cartel didn't want the people of Colombia to think that this would only be enforced in the Medellin cartel's stronghold. The new rule applied to everywhere and everyone. No one was too far away for the kingpins to reach. And it didn't take long for MAS to show everyone that they meant business. Within just a few weeks after MAS' official announcement, dozens upon dozens of M-19 militants were captured, tortured, beaten, interrogated, and slaughtered, all in an effort to retrieve Marta Ochoa and punish M-19 for their suicidal audacity. The carnage was so bad that M-19 actually had a recruitment crisis, and their numbers were taking a considerable hit. Around the middle of February 1982, Marta Ochoa was finally released unharmed. M-19 simply couldn't keep up with the cartel's attacks.

The fact that M-19, a powerful insurgency military group, had just bowed to what were basically a bunch of drug dealers was huge. It was a true testament to how powerful the cartel had become, especially considering that M-19 could not even be defeated by the Colombian government. Not even the country's military could defeat M-19, but the cartels forced them to surrender in a matter of weeks. Pablo and Jorge Ochoa's men had even kidnapped M-19's top commander in Antioquia, and the Colombian military had been after him for *years*. If the cartels could so easily do what the military could not, what would this mean for the future of Colombia? By 1982, the Medellin cartel had fully solidified itself as the premiere military narcotic organization in the country and, perhaps, the entire world. With a combination of power, money, and a ruthless reputation, Pablo Escobar had entrenched himself as its unquestioned leader. Men like Jorge Ochoa and Jose Gacha were indeed powerful and richer than anyone on earth had any right to be, but Pablo Escobar was like a god walking among men.

Death of A Minister

After 1981, anything seemed possible. Specifically for Pablo, his wildest dreams seemed easily attainable, and one of his wildest dreams was a career in politics. At this stage, it was a natural next step. He'd had strong left-wing political leanings since he was young, and he had a political ambition that mirrored his drug career. Plus, being in a position to affect policy would have been a massive benefit for the cartel's business. Pablo had cultivated a beloved public image for himself, especially among the poor. He always avoided victimizing the impoverished and he spent millions on schools, new schoolyard renovations, and other public works to benefit the underclass. He was a very popular figure, and building a large voter base did not seem out of the question. So, in 1982, he decided to leverage his fame and admiration within Antioquia to run for a local office.

Pablo campaigned for a seat in Colombia's Congress, and although he did not get exactly what he wanted, he did have enough voters to win an alternate seat. This meant, that in the event the congressman ahead of him was unable to perform his duties, it was Pablo Escobar that would take his role. He had firmly implanted himself into national politics, but an alternate seat was as close as Pablo would ever come to his Presidential aspirations. Regardless, he used his new political status to great effect, and he acquired many allies within Colombia's center-left wing Liberal Party. His personal politics aligned well with many of the more radical and progressive congressmen, and they weren't exactly eager to turn down the resources of one of the richest men in the country. He had gathered more important connections than ever before. He also had far less to fear from Colombian law enforcement because, aside from political connections, Pablo also gained congressional immunity. This meant that Pablo could not be prosecuted by his fellow Congress members, which stymied the efforts of the Colombian government to take him down. He was more invulnerable than ever before.

Unfortunately for Pablo, his new political position also put him on the map in a serious way. Now, all of his exploits would be worthy of international news, as he now became widely recognized as a crooked congressional gunslinger who pushed cocaine into the U.S. Now, Griselda Blanco could not serve as a shield for him, and he was on the radar of every American anti-narcotic organization, including the FBI, the CIA, and the Bureau of Alcohol, Tobacco, and Firearms (ATF). The wake of Pablo's election to Congress coincided with a sharp increase in attention and involvement of American legal agencies that would only get worse as Pablo's notoriety grew. This was far from a deterrent, though. Pablo openly challenged both the American and Colombian governments, and although he feared the possibility of being extradited to the United States, there was very little he needed to worry about so long as he held congressional immunity.

Pablo didn't just propel his own political power in 1982. The Panamanian military strongman Manuel Noriega had been a friend and close ally of Pablo Escobar for some time, and in 1982, they signed a deal together to allow the transportation of mass amounts of Pablo's cocaine through Panama (which was directly north of Colombia) for a fee. The fee was paid directly to Noriega, and as Pablo consistently pushed hundreds and hundreds of kilos of cocaine through the country, the general was able to amass a fortune. He had profited so greatly from the Escobar deal that he was able to propel himself to national prominence. He became one of the country's most powerful men, which he leveraged into becoming the ruler of the nation in 1983. Before long, Pablo would have to call in his favor.

Pablo now had the ear of some of the most influential men in the country, but unfortunately, it didn't take long for his fellow congressmen and politicians to turn on him. In the summer of 1983, a Medellin superior court judge formally filed a petition to have Congressman Escobar stripped of his immunity so that he could be prosecuted for the trafficking crimes they had long suspected him of. The prime motivation behind the support to have Pablo's immunity taken was the fact that Pablo was now considered the only realistic culprit behind the murders of DAS agents Vasco and Hernandez. Once again, the whole affair was coming back to haunt Pablo. The more strident of his colleagues openly called for his arrest, and in October of 1983, an official arrest warrant was issued. It turned out to be more of a formality, though, as Pablo was *still* immune from prosecution.

His luck soon ran out. Later that month, Pablo had his congressional immunity revoked, and the legal and political onslaught against him began. Things were looking grim, and attacks were coming from all angles. His friends were still doing what they could to protect him, but the top echelon of the government had decided that enough was enough. He needed to go to prison. Pablo quickly became a fugitive in his own country, and he resorted to hiding out at his Hacienda Napoles estate outside of Medellin. The place was a veritable fortress with several escape routes and extremely high security. If the police dared to descend on the mansion grounds, Pablo would have more than enough warning to escape.

The hunt was intensified after March 1984 when Colombian authorities discovered two massive drug compounds in the Yari jungle. One was in Tranquilandia and the other in Villacoca. The properties were huge and equipped with fully functioning power grids, as well as runways for launching cargo planes stocked with cocaine destined for Panama or Florida. The properties' valuables were promptly seized or destroyed, and the Colombian Minister of Justice Rodrigo Lara Bonilla formally accused Pablo Escobar and Jose Gonzalo Gacha of being the owners of the labs. Pablo was made even more vulnerable, and he was outraged at Lara's inability to be bought off with bribes or threats. On top of that, Lara publicly named Pablo as a villainous drug lord that profited from selling poison. Before long, Pablo decided that he needed to die.

Lara Bonilla was Minister of Justice under President Belisario Betancur, whose career was based on establishing peace with groups like M-19 and FARC. Lara, though, was a lawyer at heart, and his ambition was to eliminate the undue cartel influence in Colombian political and social life. To him, men like Pablo were a plague, and the fact that these men possessed resources that rivaled the government itself was a national embarrassment.

For Lara's efforts to combat this, he had sealed his own fate. In April of 1984, as Pablo was hiding in his compound, Lara was gunned down inside his car in Bogota. Everyone immediately assumed Pablo Escobar was behind it. Even the poor, who had long been his base of support, knew it was him. His death had sparked a massive war between the government and the drug cartels as President Betancur announced that he would take swift and aggressive action. He also announced that he would begin the process of extraditing the cocaine kingpins to the United States, something that Pablo, Jorge Ochoa, and others had feared for years.

Since the man who murdered Lara had been successfully captured by police, and because it seemed like the entire country knew Pablo was responsible, he knew it was time to leave. Even Hacienda Napoles wasn't safe enough. For the first time in his life, Pablo was unwillingly forced out of his native Colombia.

CHAPTER 5

A MAN ON THE RUN

Pablo Escobar and his allies had become adept at avoiding legal problems, but things were quickly getting much more complicated. His run for political office had backfired on him in a major way; though he had become a household name in Colombia and the United States, his Congressional immunity ultimately meant nothing as the entire effort was for naught. Staying under the radar, which had done so much to boost Pablo's success early on, was now an outdated concept. He was a public enemy, an infamous ne'er-do-well with a penchant for indiscriminate violence. The government of Belisario Betancur was throwing every resource they had at taking down the man who killed one of his top cabinet Ministers. Pablo could no longer rely on the mechanisms he had built to protect himself. There was no shortage of places he could run, but unfortunately, those safe havens turned out to not be safe for very long.

Exile

When Pablo deemed Hacienda Napoles unsafe, he first fled to one of his safehouses in his hometown of Envigado. This was a wise decision, because shortly after he fled, government agents raided his compound and seized millions of dollars in property. Several more millions were seized at his other properties in Medellin and throughout Antioquia. This was a huge hit, but Pablo was smart enough not to pile his resources in one location. By strategically spreading his wealth around in different accounts across various countries, he ensured that the Colombian state could only do so much to cripple the organization. And since he wasn't behind bars, he was still free to run his organization through proxies. As long as Pablo could keep the cocaine flowing through the country, he could continue to line his pockets.

But, after the raids, Pablo knew it would only be a matter of time before he was found. Every time he changed his location, he was taking the risk of being recognized in public, and his hometown would not exactly be low on the list of places the police would check. Pablo still had enough connections within the city to get tipoffs from the local cops, but the government had resorted to using mostly out-of-towners because they were hesitant to trust most of the Medellin natives, rightly believing they could be compromised. If Pablo was going to be caught, it was going to be a blindside. So long as he remained in Colombia, he would be looking over his shoulder daily for the government search squads. He decided to smuggle himself out of the country, but where could he go? The answer lay with Manuel Noriega, Pablo's friend who had recently become the military dictator of Panama. He boarded one of his secret planes that carried him over the northern border into Panama, where he was greeted with all the amenities he had become accustomed to.

In Panama, Pablo was under direct protection by the Panama government and was given whatever he needed to continue to administer his drug empire. He dictated orders back to his underlings in Medellin, but most of the partners were also absent from the country. Rodriguez Gacha and the Ochoa brothers were all government targets, and they were forced to accompany Pablo to Panama for safety. Carlos Lehder also fled. Pablo's deal with Panama was lucrative for everyone involved, but he still did not feel like he was out of the woods yet. Noriega's loyalty and cooperation only went so far as it benefitted him. But he had problems of his own. No matter how much financial support he received from the cartels, his entire political career was contingent on maintaining good relations with the United States. Cartel support would do little to offset an American invasion, and the Americans were no strangers to overthrowing foreign governments that had worn out their patience. Noriega had been caught in illegal weapon sales by American officials, and although he was not facing international charges, he was beginning to worry. And Pablo had completely lost confidence in him.

Pablo started putting some of Noriega's top lieutenants on his payroll so that he could keep tabs on the President's movements. He also put a contingency plan in place. He had already started to form connections with the Sandinista National Liberation Front, a political movement in Nicaragua, and since they had come to power in 1979, Pablo had another potential hideout in mind. While still in Panama, he began negotiations with the Sandinista President Daniel Ortega to allow Pablo property, resources, and airfield access in the country so that he could continue to funnel cocaine into America. In return, Pablo would pay millions to the Sandinistas, who used the cash flow to secure the future of their young revolution.

At some point in 1984, Pablo discovered what he had feared all along. Noriega had been communicating with American officials and was planning on betraying Pablo, selling him out to the Americans in return for immunity and a guarantee that he wouldn't be deposed or imprisoned. That was the signal Pablo was waiting for, and shortly afterwards, he and the other cartel partners fled further north to Nicaragua.

The opportunity in Nicaragua promised even more profitability than the old Panama arrangement. The Sandinistas were already on poor terms with the United States, so there was little chance of Ortega or his comrades cooperating with them against Pablo, who was now one of the only sources of funding the country could secure due to U.S. economic sanctions. Plus, the power and influence of the Sandinistas seemed to be growing, while that of Noriega was rapidly diminishing. Pablo and his associates landed in the Nicaraguan capital city of Managua where they met with Sandinista officials. They arranged for Pablo to be taken to his accommodations and to the properties he would have access to. Pablo and the Ochoas quickly got to work redirecting their shipping routes to fly through their new nodes in Nicaragua. With unlimited access to private airports, Pablo was able to saturate the American market even while in exile. Still using labs in Medellin and in Panama to process the coca paste into powder, Pablo had the product routed through clandestine Nicaraguan airports, and from there, they poured into America.

A fundamental aspect of this plan remaining profitable was the pilots that the cartel employed. Without the actual trained pilots flying the aircraft, the flow of cocaine would slow to a crawl, and that had the potential of ruining Pablo and his organization. On top of the constant fear of extradition to the United States, the drug lords also had to worry about their airmen deciding to flip on them.

There's no doubt that the pilots were on the frontline of the cocaine war, and if there was a big bust, it was usually the pilots who would be the first ones to go down, since their vehicles carried tons of illegal substances. Unfortunately, by the start of 1984, one of their most important pilots was already compromised. Barry Seal was about 10 years Pablo's senior and was a native of Louisiana. He was an experienced aircraft pilot and had flown commercially before deciding to get involved in the smuggling business. By 1976, he was flying shipments of marijuana across the United States, and a few years later, he upgraded to cocaine. In 1981, he was working closely with the Medellin Cartel. He had developed extensive connections, particularly with the Ochoa Family and with Los Pablos, but he was also unknowingly being monitored by the DEA.

The DEA and FBI were aware of Seal's smuggling activities, but not of the depth of his involvement with Pablo's cartel. In March of 1983, as part of the increasing onslaught against the cocaine lords, Seal was officially indicted along with over 70 other pilot smugglers. In less than a month, Seal willingly surrendered himself to American authorities with the intention of securing an immunity deal in exchange for information. Unfortunately, his pleas were refused and he eventually stood trial in 1984. In a last-ditch effort, he reached out to the office of the Drug Task Force, which was run by Ronal Reagan's Vice President George H. W. Bush, one of the nation's premiere anti-drug crusaders. The Task Force was less inclined to brush off valuable information, and once they learned how involved Seal was in the Ochoa Family business, they were desperate to learn what he knew. Before long, Seal had signed an official deal with the DEA to serve as an informant against Pablo and the Ochoas. And Seal was motivated to fulfill his new duties because his eventual sentence was contingent on how valuable his information turned out to be.

Over the next several months, Seal began compiling a lot of damning information about Pablo and the cartel, and he even gathered video evidence using hidden cameras planted in the planes that he piloted for Pablo. The DEA's real hope, though, was to get Seal to convince Pablo to come to the United States. Although the Colombian government constantly threatened to extradite drug dealers, they had always been reluctant to go through with it because it was generally an unpopular policy among Colombians. So, if they couldn't have Pablo sent to them, the next best thing would be to trick him into coming voluntarily. If they could catch him stateside, they could hit him with a life sentence and watch the Medellin Cartel scramble and crumble without their big boss. Unfortunately, they never got the opportunity for their grand move, but the evidence that Seal compiled did lead to the first American indictments against Pablo Escobar and Jorge Ochoa.

Seal's treachery would not go unpunished once the cartel discovered his role, but for the time being, Pablo had more immediate problems. American pressure against Latin American governments to turn over Pablo was increasing, and both the Panamanian and Nicaraguan situations were looking grim. The U.S. military was on course to invade Panama in the coming years, and in Nicaragua, the Sandinista regime was losing considerable international standing because of their reputed support for Pablo Escobar and his associates. Indeed, Nicaragua was becoming an inhospitable environment. On top of that, Pablo and the others knew they needed to reassert themselves in the actual headquarters of the organization. Thus, he headed back to his home to reclaim his seat of power.

The Extraditables

Later in 1984, Pablo hopped on one of his secret personal aircrafts and flew out of Nicaragua, destined for Medellin's Olaya Herrera airport. After he managed to land without alerting the authorities, he quickly hopped on a helicopter and headed for his beloved Hacienda Napoles. Back in Colombia, Pablo was prepared for all-out war with the government. He was willing to fight extradition at all costs, and his associates were on board. This was particularly true of Lehder, who almost seemed to have psychosis induced by fear of extradition. The Colombian government had been endlessly pursuing "crazy Charlie" since 1979, and he was getting more aggressive by the day. Because he was already cripplingly paranoid from his cocaine addiction, he was becoming a major problem for the cartel.

The undercover work of Barry Seal had recently come to light, and due to his testimonies in court, the U.S. government was exerting even more pressure on Panama and Nicaragua to crack down on cartel activities in their countries. Pablo and the others were at risk of losing their transport nodes north of Colombia, and on top of that, the Colombian government had actually started extraditing drug criminals. By mid-1985, half a dozen Colombian traffickers had been shipped to the United States for trial, and another nine were sitting in prison awaiting the same fate. If Pablo was captured, he would almost certainly be put on the fast track to extradition, and the same went for Ochoa, Rodriguez Gacha, and Lehder. Ochoa had actually been on the lam in Spain at the time, and after Seal's testimonies, all of the major Colombian cocaine smugglers, including Ochoa, had arrest warrants issued against them by a

Florida court. In late 1984, Ochoa was captured as a result of the American warrant but was not yet sent back either to Colombia nor the U.S. As more Colombians were being targeted, Pablo's group publicly stated that, for every Colombian shipped off to the U.S., ten judges would be hunted and executed.

Knowing Pablo, everyone took this threat at face value. He had already proven that he was not above killing cops, judges, and even high-ranking politicians to get what he wanted. And what he wanted most was a Constitutional ban on extradition. It was really the only thing that would guarantee the doom of Pablo's organizations, so this was a hill he was willing to die on. Sources differ on exactly when, but at some point in late 1984 or early 1985, in the Antioquian town of Girardota, a huge meeting was called to gather most of the major remaining drug lords. All of the men in attendance were obvious targets of extradition for the government, and at this meeting, they agreed on the formation of a group known as "The Extraditables." The Extraditables was a political and military organization with the express goal of intimidating the government of President Betancur into passing laws making extradition illegal. Unlike the MAS paramilitary organization that the cartel created to combat kidnapping, The Extraditables was a sophisticated group that didn't rely solely on violence. They actively lobbied political parties to oppose extradition on a Constitutional level, and even crafted slogans and mottos like the catchy "Say No to Extradition!" and the not so catchy "Better a grave in Colombia than a jail cell in the U.S." Still, though, their most powerful weapon was intimidation and bloodshed.

The Extraditables, whose military wing was headed by Pablo and Rodriguez Gacha, soon began targeting proponents of extradition.

Before he could give his full attention to his renewed terror campaign, though, he had an important personal matter to settle with his ex-pilot Barry Seal. He was about to make another example of the price of disloyalty. He decided that Seal needed to die. He smuggled Colombian assassins into the United States to track down and murder the informant. It was easier said than done, though, and it took quite a while before Pablo's plan could actually come to fruition. The time finally came in 1986 when they finally tracked him down, at which point they could formulate a plan to get to him. Seal had been relatively lax with his security, believing he would be safe from the cartel in his hometown of Baton Rouge, but underestimating the reach of the cartel was usually a fatal mistake. On February 19, Seal was gunned down, and Pablo could rest easy knowing he had gotten revenge. Unfortunately, the gunmen ran into bad luck after the hit. Just minutes after they had sped away from the crime scene, they were pulled over for a minor traffic violation. Literally just as the officer that stopped them was trying desperately to communicate with the Colombian natives, the report of Seal's murder was announced over the radio. The officer put two and two together and pulled his gun, arresting the two gunmen. Given the fact of who Seal was and the fact that the men they captured were Colombian, everyone knew immediately Pablo was behind the murder that had just taken place.

While the hunt for Seal was still underway, Pablo was getting busy acquiring the phone numbers, addresses, and personal details of judges and politicians all over Colombia. On a daily basis, justices were being telephoned at home and having their lives and the lives of their families threatened. If they went ahead in supporting an extradition treaty, they were putting their wives and children at risk.

Letters were sent to them both at home and at work, with messages threatening kidnap and torture. One letter stated, "We declare war against you. We declare war against your families" (Attwood, 2016). The letter, moreover, was signed by The Extraditables. To instill fear, they would often call judges and tell them details about their personal lives to show how much they knew. They would recite their daily schedules back to them and advise that they stop being so predictable. In one case, a judge had taken his daughter to the hospital for surgery, and just as she was taken in, a representative of The Extraditables phoned the hospital, spoke with the judge, and told him that they knew exactly where she was.

The standoff between the Medellin Cartel and the Colombian government was heating up in a dangerous way. Since the beginning of the fiasco, the cartel was responding with violence. In late November of 1984, just days after President Betancur finally began signing the first extradition orders, a car bomb exploded directly outside the American embassy in Bogota. This was where American delegates had been meeting with Colombian officials to discuss the extradition treaty. The blast killed a female bystander and five others were hospitalized. Just over a week prior to this, several American diplomats were evacuated from that very building because they had been receiving threatening messages. This was just the beginning, though. The 1984 embassy bombing was not the last nor the greatest of Pablo's terrorist activities, and Barry Seal would not be the last of Pablo's enemies to die in a hail of gunfire. As we'll see, this was only the tip of the iceberg of what Pablo Escobar was willing to do to avoid being sent to America.

CHAPTER 6

PABLO ESCOBAR: INTERNATIONAL TERRORIST

With Pablo Escobar's continued violent attacks against the government and his stubborn refusal to stop funneling cocaine into America, he had become an internationally wanted man. Colombian justices of the highest courts in the country were living in fear. Both they and their families were being threatened with torture and death, and for a time, it genuinely seemed like Colombia could descend into a state bordering civil war. Needless to say, his exploits were becoming intolerable to both the Colombian and American governments.

Black November

One day in 1985, while Pablo and the remaining drug lords were engaged in their war against the government, some distinguished guests came to visit the kingpin at his Hacienda Napoles fortress. The men were important generals in the M-19 guerrilla army, the same group that the cartel had decimated after the formation of MAS (Death to Kidnappers). Despite their rocky history, Pablo was actually quite ideologically aligned with M-19. He had a strong political mind that often guided his business life, but the massacre in response to Marta Ochoa's kidnapping was compartmentalized as a purely business matter. Aside from that, he was sympathetic to the group. Plus, they had a common enemy in Betancur's government. As for M-19, they were operating under a "the enemy of my enemy is my friend" mindset, and with Pablo's resources at their disposal, perhaps they could finally turn the tables on the government.

To that end, the generals had an intriguing offer for Pablo. As it turned out, they had been planning to stage a grand assault on the Colombian Palace of Justice in Bogota. The audacious plan involved storming the main building and attempting to force the President into facing trial in hopes of potentially seizing control of the government. In addition, M-19 was also strongly against the extradition of Colombians as a matter of nationalist principle, so the attack was going to be partially in service of that. It also made Pablo Escobar a natural ally in the cause. Pablo was also generally open to the idea of furthering M-19's political goals, so he wasn't quick to refuse them. So, the M-19 generals told Pablo that their planned siege would be beneficial for them both. They asked the drug lord if he would be willing to fund the military venture.

Pablo mulled over the offer, likely while puffing on a joint, and eventually agreed to their terms. Not only did Pablo offer up roughly $1 million in cash to the insurgency group, but he also gave them indefinite access to his storage facilities and his plane yards, should the need for them arise. Pablo was always willing to go big, and this occasion was no different. Besides, Betancur had proved to be exactly the kind of treacherous snake Pablo thought he was. A focal point of his campaign was to create a lasting peace in the country with the many guerilla groups, but in the wake of their supposed "peace deal" with M-19, his army had continued assaults and air strikes against their rural bases. Betancur was, as far as Pablo and the generals were concerned, far from a champion of peace. He was a nuisance that should be disposed of, if given the chance. The best-case scenario was that M-19 would actually force the Colombian courts to try the President in a court of law for his criminal refusal to abide by the peace he had signed. This was, to put it mildly, a long shot, but even the worst-case scenario was that the guerillas would strike fear once again into the hearts of every Colombian judge and politician, reminding them that they were not the only strong force in the country. For Pablo, it was a no-lose situation, and it was worth a measly $1 million, an amount he would make back in cocaine sales before the night was through.

So, the wheels were in motion. In early November, M-19 began making moves to ensure that the Palace of Justice takeover would be a swift one. Secret M-19 soldiers dressed in civilian and government clothing quietly entered the Palace on the night of November 5, bringing small arms with them. They hid and lay in wait for their comrades who were meant to join them in the morning. What followed remains one of the most infamous days in Colombian history. On November 6, the primary assault force drove to the Palace and arrived just before noon. Truckloads of guerrillas were dropped off right in front of the main entrance, heavily armed with assault rifles and explosives. The exterior security was unprepared, and the guerrillas quickly shot the guards dead before they could do anything. They swept into the main building, gunning down those that tried to flee in the chaos. They moved quickly to lock down the entire building and prevent anyone from leaving—the more hostages they could get, the better. The guerrillas took innocent civilians as hostages, including low-level employees, as well as justices, lawyers, and other legal dignitaries. By the time the siege was in full effect, some 300 individuals were being held captive by M-19 (Atwood, 2016).

As the M-19 attackers were mowing down government employees trying to escape from the Palace, the nation was plunged into chaos and fear. Colombians in faraway cities and the countryside didn't know the extent of what was going on. Was this only the beginning? If the Palace of Justice could so easily be captured, would more attacks be coming? Some began to worry that a full coup of the Colombian government was imminent. These fears weren't totally unwarranted. President Betancur was deeply troubled himself. He was at once shocked, embarrassed, and infuriated. He was panicking, and the only thing he could think to do was send in the military. The only problem was that most of the military's ranks were simply inexperienced at dealing with situations like these. Delicate situations that involved hostage negotiation and avoidance of collateral damage were a far cry from raining hell on jungle hideouts. Nevertheless, Betancur gave them a blank cheque to do whatever they deemed necessary to retake the Palace from M-19.

The next day, the soldiers were prepared to make their move. The guerrillas had so far failed in getting Betancur to stand down the army and negotiate, and it didn't appear likely that he would give in to a single one of their demands. As the guerrillas continued to terrorize and execute hostages, the military was preparing to breach the building. Troops had been exchanging gunfire consistently for over 24 hours but there was little progress being made by either side. It took a tank to finally break the stalemate. It smashed into the front of the building and was followed by many dozens of government troops who poured through the massive hole the tank had created. Chaos ensued as the guerrillas scurried to take cover. In the confusion, many more hostages were killed both by M-19 and the army, as noncombatants were mistaken for rebel fighters. Eventually, though, the guerrillas were overwhelmed. They had nowhere to run, and they couldn't fight an entire army. None of the guerrillas are believed to have survived the liberation of the Palace.

On November 7, the siege was over. Civilian casualties numbered around 100, and M-19 took yet another serious blow, having lost a lot of men and huge amounts of investment in an utter failure. For Pablo, though, there was a lot to smile about, and much of that had to do with the fact that, of all the many deaths during the siege, 11 of them were sitting members of the Supreme Court. The highest judicial court in the country, the same one that had been making Pablo's life hell, had lost half of its members. Regardless of the failure, the government had been dealt a blow. It was clear to everyone that Pablo benefitted from the siege, and it took no time at all for Betancur and Minister of Justice Enrique Parejo (whose predecessor, Rodrigo Lara Bonilla, was assassinated on Pablo's orders) to publicly accuse Pablo of being behind the entire Palace siege. The assumption that Pablo Escobar had funded the bold operation was supported by the fact that, during the siege, the guerrilla soldiers also took the time to find and burn hundreds of copies of documents relating to the Medellin Cartel and the extradition orders for top drug criminals. Profiles of major traffickers were destroyed, as were other important legal papers. The real impact of this gesture was limited because most of the burned files had copies in other government filing systems, but the real purpose was to send a message, warning the government to get off the cartel's back.

In the aftermath of the Palace Siege, the government was in complete disarray. The top Colombian court was crippled, and government employees were now afraid to do their jobs. Many judges who managed to keep their lives after the massacre ended up quitting law shortly after. Part of this was out of fear, but it was also largely out of anger toward Betancur and his refusal to negotiate. The popular take was that Betancur's aggressive yet delayed reaction caused many more deaths than otherwise would have happened. The "guns blazing" style of resolution that took place on the 7th put the innocent hostages right in the middle of the shootout and many were used as human shields that the army soldiers didn't hesitate to blast through. For all the people who died that day and all who lost loved ones, the President's symbolic and principled stance on not negotiating with terrorists meant very little. Betancur, on top of his seething anger, was losing standing and respect. He couldn't let this slide.

Still, the only strategy Betancur deemed viable was more violence. The army and police forces reacted brutally, and the streets of Medellin and the other major Colombian cities were soon flooded with blood yet again. In reality, there were not really any alternative courses of action for Betancur. After November 6, how could the cartel possibly be reasoned with? How could the government ever coexist with an organization that just assaulted the very infrastructure of Colombian law? So, it was war. Throughout Medellin, cops, soldiers, and cartel hitmen were having open shootouts in the streets. Gunmen were dropping dead left and right, and a curfew was put in effect for all citizens of Medellin. If you were caught outside after dark, it would have been safe to assume you were a combatant. Day after day, police and Pablo's men were in direct conflict. That month, nicknamed "Black November," was a dark period in Colombia's history. The leadership of M-19 was decimated during the siege and the rest of Black November, but the Medellin Cartel remained a formidable and resourceful adversary. The bloody siege was an aggressive warning to the proponents of extradition that the cartel would stop at absolutely nothing to avoid the United States.

The Bloodbath

By 1986, the Medellin Cartel and the Colombian government were in a direct and escalating conflict. President Betancur was in an impossible position, and the end of his political career seemed to be rapidly approaching. On November 13, 1985, just one week after the siege on the Palace of Justice, a massive volcanic eruption happened in the Department of Tolima, which fully engulfed the town of Armara, killing almost all of its citizens. 20,000 Armarans were killed in a hail of fire and volcanic flow, and while it may have seemed like a sudden tragedy that couldn't have been helped, Colombians placed the blame for the national tragedy squarely on the Betancur government. As it turned out, Betancur had been warned by Colombian scientists months ago that the Nevado del Ruiz volcano was becoming active again and that the surrounding area should be evacuated immediately. Exactly nothing was done to prepare for the eruption, and Betancur paid the price in the court of public opinion. Not only had he failed spectacularly in his campaign goal to establish peace, but he had also failed to curb the power of the drug cartels. Now, he had failed to protect his own people from an easily preventable natural disaster. Meanwhile, Pablo Escobar was laughing.

Betancur, who was once lauded as a revolution in Colombian politics, had become a laughingstock by the end of the year. He claimed that peace would reign between the government and the guerrilla groups, but instead, they took over one of the most important government buildings and slew half of the Supreme Court. He also had once claimed that the smugglers, whom he referred to as the "bad sons of Colombia," (Smith, 2018) would find the new Colombia to be quite an inhospitable environment. Instead, they thrived and openly challenged the state military. When Minister of Justice Rodrigo Lara Bonilla was gunned down by Pablo's hitmen, he claimed that their "national dignity was held hostage by the smugglers" and that he would soon extradite them en masse (Smith, 2018). Instead, shortly after the Palace of Justice siege, Colombian lawmakers gave in to the pressure of constant death threats and ruled extradition to the United States to be unconstitutional. All of this combined to ruin Betancur's national standing and prestige. The year 1986 would be his last as President.

Although the court ruling was a win for Pablo, it was not a done deal. The incoming Presidency of Virgilio Barco Vargas was worrying, and the man seemingly had no intention of holding true to the ruling, which did not take place under his rule. Set to take the Presidential office in August, Barco seemed to take a reconciliatory stance toward the left-wing guerrilla groups but a more hardline approach toward the drug lords. As a result, the violence that had plagued Colombian cities was about to grow considerably, and the hunt for Pablo would be exacerbated. As always, it would be innocent Colombian civilians who would be caught in the middle of all of it. Some even believed that, after the Palace siege, the Colombian military had actually taken control of the government and both Betancur and the incoming Barco had become mere puppets of the military. War was on the mind of every Colombian. Betancur had made the state apparatus appear impotent, and if even they could not protect Colombians, who could?

As Barco was gaining renown for his brutal rhetoric against the drug cartels, Pablo was becoming more frantic and much more violent. His hit squads were wantonly attacking government agencies and structures, and he was planning the most audacious murder plots and acts of terror, including more car bombings and public executions. Every Colombian politician at nearly every level of government, was mortally terrified of the possibility of becoming Pablo's next target. With half of the Supreme Court murdered, it proved very difficult to replace the slain justices. One new Supreme Court justice, a newcomer named Fernando Uribe, resigned from his post just months after taking it. He was receiving constant death threats and threatening phone calls, and his dedication to upholding the law suddenly appeared inconsequential next to his own personal safety and the safety of his family.

The man who replaced Uribe went through the exact same thing and also resigned in the same way. Supreme Court justice Hernando Borda, who had been serving since February of 1985, managed to survive the onslaught at the Palace of Justice, and he wasn't afraid enough to resign like so many others. But he paid the price sooner rather than later. He was one of the original drafters of the Colombia-U.S. extradition treaty, and in late July of 1986, he was murdered in a drive-by shooting that was ordered by Pablo Escobar. Headed to the Supreme Court, his family car was ambushed by gunmen who shot him and his wife, forced him out of the car, and executed him on the streets of the capital Bogota.

Pablo had a lot on his plate in 1986. The government, despite its many blows and defeats, was continuing to persecute the cartels. But Pablo also had more internal issues to deal with, ones that hit close to home. Carlos Lehder, the helplessly cocaine-addicted co-founder of the Medellin Cartel, was becoming a huge problem. Years earlier, the Colombian government had seized all of his assets and frozen his accounts, cutting him off almost completely from his massive wealth. The former billionaire was now dirt poor, and he resorted to going on the run in the Colombian jungle, hiding out in caves and antagonizing the government with video footage in which he claimed he would never give up the fight against the government tyrants. He was also basically a neo-Nazi and had been even more militant than Pablo was, which was drawing a lot of unnecessary heat.

At one point, Pablo's sentimental and compassionate side took over, and he extracted Lehder from the jungle and took him back to Medellin where he served Pablo as a familiar, if unreliable, bodyguard. It was a major step down for the former superstar smuggler, but he had not yet hit rock bottom. His drug-fueled tirades about waging civil war and seizing control of Colombia were off-putting to Pablo, and before long, the Medellin don had had enough. He had taken Lehder, who was very vulnerable, under his direct protection, but was repaid only with more insanity and incoherent plans for some kind of new Colombian society. Government assaults were one thing, but Lehder's mental instability could realistically have dismantled the Medellin business.

In 1987, Lehder was set up at a farm near the Antioquian town of Guarne. While he was there, Pablo decided that loyalty to friends really did have its limits. He willingly gave up his location to the Colombian government, possibly as part of some kind of deal whereby Pablo would offer up scapegoats in return for lax treatment. Lehder, who had trusted Pablo to help him get his life back on track, had been sold out by him instead. Colombian police received Pablo's tipoff about the ranch house and descended swiftly on him. He was taken into police custody and, in less than a day, he was being processed to be deported from the country back to the United States to face trial. The Americans had been wanting to get their hands on Lehder for years, and because of Pablo, they would very soon have their way. He was on a plane destined for America within hours, and there, he would find few sympathetic ears. Even if the American Supreme Court justices were willing to overlook his past, they were not willing to overlook what information he knew.

So, although Pablo solved the problem, Lehder had the potential to be even more destructive while in government custody. Lehder was one of the Medellin Cartel's most influential founding fathers, and the Americans wanted to learn everything they could from him. Not content with the damage he had already done, Lehder contributed significantly to the eventual downfall of the Medellin Cartel while in America. Aside from that, Lehder's absence also meant that his entire faction of the Medellin Cartel was now either fully destroyed or in complete disarray, which made the rest of the cartel leaders less powerful and less wealthy. The reward that Lehder got for his cooperation also sent a stern reminder to the remaining drug lords that extradition was just a fancy word for "the end." In 1988, Carlos

Lehder was read his sentence, which included over 100 years in federal prison with no possibility of parole or early release.

Lehder wasn't the only cartel founder who was in a more than precarious position. Jorge Ochoa, who was now back in Colombia after having been extradited from Spain in the summer of 1986, was also facing a massive campaign waged by the Americans to have him extradited stateside. Before any decisions were made, though, Ochoa was handed a suspended sentence for his arrest in Spain, meaning he was allowed to walk free so long as he followed terms of probation. Shortly after, though, Ochoa disappeared but was captured yet again in late November of 1987, and calls to extradite him were renewed. The new Colombian Minister of Justice Enrique Low, who served under new President Barco Vargas, was also lobbying aggressively for the court to unanimously agree on extradition for drug traffickers. In doing so, Low made himself Pablo's newest hit target.

After the Lehder affair, it seemed almost certain that Ochoa would be extradited as well, although it was still a heated topic in the courts. But shortly after he was apprehended, a letter signed by "The Extraditables" was submitted to the newspaper *El Colombiano* that claimed they would stage a massive assassination campaign against Colombian politicians and lawmakers all over the country if Jorge Luis Ochoa were indeed extradited to America. After the Palace of Justice affair, absolutely no one thought that this was a bluff. The Colombian courts already had a cloud of violence over their heads, and unlike Enrique Low, who was also a survivor of the Palace of Justice slaughter, most justices were starting to bend to this pressure. By the end of 1987, Ochoa was released from captivity.

Ochoa's release did very little to curb the tide of cartel violence against the government, though. In January of 1988, Medellin Cartel thugs kidnapped Andres Pastrana Arango, frontrunner for the Bogota mayoral election and future President of Colombia, from his campaign headquarters. He was held captive for a week before he was discovered by police. Juan Gomez, a candidate for the mayor of Medellin, had also nearly been kidnapped by the cartel earlier, but the plan was foiled. Later in January, after the Pastrana kidnapping, Pablo also ordered the abduction of Carlos Mauro Hoyos, the Attorney General of Colombia and close cooperator with the American DEA. On the 25th, as he was driving to an airport outside of Medellin, his car was stopped and both of his bodyguards were shot dead. Mauro Hoyos was shot but survived, and the gunmen whisked him off to a hideout in the city. News broke almost immediately, and the government began a frantic search. It's not clear exactly what Pablo's ultimate plan with Mauro Hoyos was, but when mayoral candidate Pastrana Arango was discovered by a search party that same day, an enraged Pablo ordered his immediate execution.

In 1988, the future that Pablo had desperately been fighting against became reality. Having had enough of the cartel's repetitive kidnappings and murders, the courts ruled in favor of extradition, and it was now in full swing in Colombia. Ochoa was already under threat after more than a couple of close calls, but now new extradition orders were being processed for Pablo Escobar, Jose Rodriguez Gacha, and several other members of the Ochoa clan. All of the orders were signed by Enrique Low, a man Pablo had wanted dead for some time now. Extradition seemed more likely than ever before, and Pablo flew into a rage, ordering the murder and kidnapping of almost anyone who opposed him. The amount of money his organization was paying out for hit contracts was astronomical, and anyone who disagreed with him was seen as an enemy. Things were quickly getting out of hand as Pablo desperately tried to cling on to his smuggling empire while simultaneously fighting an all-out war with Colombia, who had the full support of the U.S. government under the new President George H. W. Bush, a noted anti-drug crusader.

The Medellin Cartel's acts became more brazen, as did the government's. In early 1989, cartel hitmen carried out their most brutal and vicious attack yet in the town of La Rochela, Simacota in the Santander department. There, a group of federal legal employees were conducting a criminal investigation on trafficking activities in the area. On January 18, over a dozen of them were ambushed by cartel thugs. Apparently aided by members of the military who were on the cartel payroll, the hitmen assembled them together and staged a mass execution. Only three of the intended targets survived the tragedy, and once again, the government's judicial system suffered a significant blow. It appeared that being a lawyer, judge, or anything related to it, was one of the most dangerous jobs in the nation. It turned out that the attack happened under the orders of Jose Rodriguez Gacha, a man for whom the walls of justice seemed to be closing in at an alarming rate. Like Pablo, Gacha was at the end of his rope and was using the only reliable tool he had—murder—to survive. La Rochela was just the latest national tragedy, but the remainder of 1989 had even more terrible surprises in store, and the execution of 12 judiciary officials proved to be just a sample of the terrorist acts that the cartel would commit that year.

At 7:13 a.m. on the morning of November 27, Avianca Flight 203 (piloted by Jose Ossa) took off from El Dorado airport in Bogota. It was a domestic flight that was destined for Cali, and with an average flight time of just over an hour, it was as routine as could be. But, less than ten minutes into the flight, while the Boeing 727 aircraft was over 10,000 feet in the air, a bomb hidden near the plane's fuel tank was detonated. In seconds, flames engulfed the cabin, and a secondary explosion literally tore the plane in two. The flaming wreckage plummeted from the sky and burning metal and fuselage rained down on the people below. There were over 100 passengers on Avianca flight 203, and each one of them died in the explosion, including the man who set off the bomb in the first place. Three more civilians were killed from the hail of the destroyed plane. Government agencies rapidly conducted investigations into the disaster, but at the time, it wasn't obvious that it was caused by anything other than a catastrophic malfunction. After the investigations concluded, there was no question about it. The explosion was intentional, and Pablo Escobar was the number one suspect. It was determined that the man who set off the bomb was paid by the Medellin Cartel, but he thought he was actually starting a recording device when he unknowingly pressed the detonator. The man who actually planted the bomb had gotten far away from the plane before it took off, leaving only their patsy holding the trigger to die in the blast.

Avianca Flight 203 was actually a passenger short the day it exploded. The candidate favored to win the upcoming Colombian national presidential elections, a man named Cesar Augusto Gaviria Trujillo, was supposed to be aboard the plane on November 27; apparently, he had a change of plans and cancelled at the last minute. The bomb hiding above the Boeing's fuel tank was meant for him. With the list of "usual suspects" getting shorter and shorter these days and the fact that Gaviria Trujillo was a primary opponent of Pablo Escobar's cartel, it was no stretch of the imagination to claim that Escobar was behind the bombing. And indeed, it turned out to be true that Pablo gave the go-ahead. Unfortunately for him, though, the presidential candidate was not harmed. Instead, over 100 innocent people lost their lives and an entire nation was terrorized.

After the Avianca attack, the hunt for Pablo Escobar absolutely exploded. This was arguably the most shocking act Pablo had committed as head of the Medellin Cartel, as it showed that he was more than willing to throw hundreds of innocents into the meat grinder just to have a *chance* at hitting the man they wanted dead. Plus, two American nationals were killed on the flight explosion along with the others, and as far as the Bush administration was concerned, that made Pablo's terrorism flagrantly international. The tragedy led to Bush ordering the U.S. Army launch Intelligence Support Activity within Colombia to aid in the capture of Pablo. This marked the most significant American involvement in the country since the Medellin Cartel first became a threat. Units of CIA agents were en route to Colombia to provide direct intelligence support, along with the American counterterrorism task force known as Delta Force. Another group that specialized in technology services, known as Centra Spike, was also sent to Colombia. Their contribution to the great hunt would be groundbreaking.

In many ways, the Avianca bombing marked the beginning of the end for Pablo's empire. With the full dedication of American involvement, his days seemed numbered. Despite that, it was not even the last tragedy of 1989. Pablo was still not willing to accept defeat, and he still commanded enough resources to launch devastating attacks against the state. Barely a week after the failed attempt to assassinate Cesar Gaviria Trujillo, Pablo took aim at the DAS, the federal security agency that had been harassing Pablo since at least the mid-1970s. In the early hours of December 6, men working for Pablo Escobar quietly drove a truck up through the southwest quarter of Bogota and parked in front of the DAS headquarters. Abandoning the vehicle there, the men left on foot. The situation in itself was not all that suspicious—Bogota in the early morning often had bumper-to-bumper traffic, and large industrial trucks parked on the roadside wasn't unusual. However, this truck was packed with roughly 1,000 pounds of dynamite. At exactly 7:30 in the morning, the dynamite was detonated, and a massive explosive blast consumed a large portion of the block. Part of the DAS building was damaged, and the collateral damage was horrific. Over 50 pedestrians and government employees were killed immediately, and several more died later in the hospital. Estimates for the number of people injured range from 400 to several thousand (Long, 1989). The massive blast had blown out windows several blocks away, and everyone in Bogota heard the explosion, causing panic throughout the city. Nothing was left of the blast site besides a huge crater and rubble in front of the DAS building.

Once again, it turned out that this grand scheme was devised to target just one person. In this case, it was Miguel Alfredo Maza Marquez, Director of the DAS since 1985. Maza, like Gaviria Trujillo, was one of Pablo's most hated opponents. But again, like with the Avianca flight 203 attack, the DAS bombing failed in its ultimate goal. Maza avoided the blast completely without injury, while dozens perished. If Pablo in the 1970s and early 1980s was seen as a champion of the underclass, the man who fought against government oppression for the good of the public and the "Robin Hood of Antioquia," he was now seen as a selfish terrorist who cared little for the lives of the innocent people who got caught in his path. His public image was being dragged through the mud, and he had no one to blame but himself. The November and December attacks not only affected hundreds of Colombian families, but they were also complete failures. The United States was getting involved in a big way, and the Colombian government was resorting to any means necessary to get Pablo. And now, 'getting' Pablo no longer meant arresting him. They wanted him dead.

Heading into 1990, the walls were closing in on Pablo. He had already lost Carlos Lehder as an associate and cartel partner, and Jose Rodriguez Gacha, the man suspected to have been behind the La Rochela Massacre, was being actively hunted. On December 15, 1989, the Colombian government made their move against Gacha after learning where he was hiding. A shootout ensued, followed by a car chase involving military helicopters and armored vehicles. Freddy Rodriguez Celades, Jose Gacha's son, had already been shot dead by police. As Jose was fleeing in a car, the driver pulled over and the pair ran away on foot. Gacha was running through a field when he panicked and began firing shots from his machine gun up at the helicopter that was searching for him. His short volley did little damage, but after he fired, the chopper reared its head toward his position and unleashed a blast from its mounted high-caliber turret. The rounds tore through Gacha's body and forced him to the ground, an inch from death. A final shot to the face ended him for good. Another one of Colombia's richest men—one of the country's most notorious terrorists and most successful drug dealers—was dead. More importantly, another integral member of Pablo's Medellin Cartel was wasted. Pablo and Jorge Luis Ochoa were still at large, and the government was eager to continue their success.

The immediate future was looking grim for Pablo. If he was found, it looked like he wouldn't even have a chance to try and bribe anyone. They would be shooting first and asking questions later, and Pablo was the most isolated he had ever been. He had only his own personal crew, Los Pablos, to protect him, plus whatever remnants remained of the badly wounded Ochoa clan. Throughout the first months of the new decade, Pablo was on the run, desperately taking potshots at government personnel and facilities to try to dissuade them from pursuing him.

But then, in September of 1990, Colombian President and former assassination target Pablo, Cesar Gaviria Trujillo, announced that he would offer significantly reduced sentences to Colombian drug traffickers in exchange for their surrender to authorities. In addition, those who surrendered under these terms would not be extradited to the United States and would remain under Colombian jurisdiction. It was a controversial announcement because, to many, it appeared as just another loophole that the drug lords would be able to exploit to avoid the consequences of their crime. For people like Pablo Escobar, Jorge Ochoa, and Jose Gacha, "reduced sentences" was simply more than they deserved. Still, the government was left with few options as the onslaught of violence continued to worsen. In early 1991, Jorge Ochoa decided that his best option to avoid death was to take the government up on their offer. He surrendered to Colombian police and was taken into custody. It looked quite likely that Pablo would be the next man to surrender.

CHAPTER 7

THE DOWNFALL

By mid-1991, Pablo Escobar stood more alone than ever before. Many of his top lieutenants were either dead or had been captured, and his only reliable, high-ranking guy remaining was his brother, Roberto Escobar. Roberto had had to take on a lot more responsibilities in the cartel since August of 1990, when another of Pablo's top lieutenants, his cousin Gustavo Gaviria, was tracked down and murdered by police in his fortress compound in Medellin. After this, and especially after Ochoa's surrender, Pablo was forced to consider that he may have to lay down his arms and accept his fate. In 1990, he had begun developing a contingency plan for just such a scenario. Aside from the police, Pablo and his associates also had to worry about the onslaught from rival drug dealers, particularly the Cali Cartel who had been on the rise in recent years, seizing on the opportunity to expand while the Medellin Cartel was bogged down by the war with the government. Pablo was now no longer the one ordering assassinations; he was the one trying to avoid them.

If he was going to go down, he needed to be sure of a few things. First, he would not be sent out of the country to the United States, nor would he accept an unrealistic prison term within Colombia.

Second, he needed protection. Colombian prisons, as Pablo knew all too well, were not impenetrable, and Pablo did not want the Cali thugs to capitalize on his captivity to have him or his family assassinated. He also didn't want to give the police the opportunity to execute him at his home. To help ensure this, Pablo began preparations on a large compound that came to be known as La Catedral—his own personal luxury resort-style prison.

The Great Hunt

Fearing for his life, Pablo surrendered to authorities in June 1991, but not before striking an important deal with them. Pablo would go to prison, sure, but a man like him was not simply going to surrender all he had built. That was out of the question. As a condition of Pablo's imprisonment, he demanded to be fully isolated from the general prison population within his custom-designed La Catedral prison that overlooked the Medellin city line. The building was stocked with all of the lavish amenities that Pablo could have wanted: It had plenty of space for him to roam around, and it allowed him to enjoy many of his favorite activities to occupy his days. He would, of course, also be able to effectively manage his empire by delegating tasks to his underlings, all of whom would be able to visit him in 'prison' upon his request. One of the most important conditions of his captivity, though, was Pablo's ability to handpick the guards that would be assigned to La Catedral. In doing so, he was able to make sure that he was surrounded by *paisas* that were loyal to him and wouldn't be easily bought off to assassinate him. In addition to that, they would also be willing to put their life on the line to protect Pablo while he was under their guard. It quickly became apparent that La Catedral was not designed to keep Pablo in so much as it was designed to keep his enemies out.

Despite the fact that the deal obviously favored Pablo, the government was desperate to get him off the streets and claim a 'win' in the eyes of the public. Besides, the Colombian government at this point didn't even care all that much about letting the cartel continue trafficking cocaine, but they needed the violence and terrorism to stop. In June, Pablo was 'arrested' and sentenced to what basically amounted to house arrest in La Catedral. There, at the little vacation resort he built for himself, he would remain for a little over a year along with his brother Roberto, who was also under threat from the Cali Cartel and government death squads. During that time, the government of Colombia was being pressured by the United States to *actually* punish Escobar. American intelligence agencies saw right through the La Catedral trick, and the Colombian government was also facing embarrassment as the public became more aware of the kind of treatment Pablo enjoyed in the compound. His 'cell' was actually a massive suite with its own hot tub. There was a fully staffed bar supplied with alcohol and marijuana, and Pablo would even host parties at La Catedral's nightclub. According to Cran (1997), the guards would often joke that the prison "was not maximum security, but maximum comfort."

So, after a little over a year of Pablo being incarcerated, the government accepted that they had been duped and decided that something had to be done. Pablo Escobar, the man that had ordered the slaughter of judges, lawyers, journalists, rivals, innocent civilians, and politicians at all levels of government, could not be allowed to serve out his entire sentence in luxury. President Cesar

Gaviria ordered that the military move in to handle the transfer of Pablo Escobar to a standard maximum security state facility. The fact that the President knew that the military would be necessary to overpower the supposedly imprisoned Pablo goes to show how much power the cocaine lord still held, and how impotent his punishment was. In July. The army descended on La Catedral, ready for a potential shootout as they cornered the prisoner. But Pablo had always anticipated the government might react this way, and he always had a backup plan. During the compound's construction, he had designed an escape route that led out the back of the facility into the jungle. Plus, many of the army officers that were in charge of his transfer that day were actually on the cartel's payroll, so there wasn't really any immediate search effort after they realized Pablo and Roberto were no longer in La Catedral. The President, however, was furious that the public enemy number one had once again slipped through the nation's fingers.

So, Pablo had just escaped from his own custom prison, and he was now on the run once again. With his Hacienda Napoles compromised and La Catedral invaded, he didn't have many places to run to, and it seemed like the end of his run was quickly approaching. He still had friends, but it seemed like the rest of the world had turned on him. He still had a war to fight, and fight it he would, but his entire organization was starting to crumble around him. The manhunt for Pablo Escobar was once more reignited, and the men in charge were out for blood. There would be no deals this time. They weren't looking to capture Pablo or extradite him. Their orders were to shoot on sight, and the highly trained task forces that had been hunting Pablo since the 1980s were now more eager than ever to do it. One group in particular would make Pablo's time in hiding particularly hellish.

Back in 1986, President Virgilio Barco authorized the creation of a special and highly trained task force skilled in intelligence, espionage, and urban combat. The group received extensive training from the Colombian military and also received support from the American intelligence services. They became an elite fighting force known as the Search Bloc. Search Bloc's ranks were staffed with many who had a personal grudge against the Medellin Cartel because they had been wronged by them in some way or another, and although they contributed to the downfall of many cartel leaders, the group was created for one primary mission: Hunt down and capture Pablo Escobar. At the time the group was created, Pablo was already the subject of the government's hunt, but after the rash of terrorism and mass murder in 1989, Search Bloc was kicked into another gear altogether. The seemingly incorruptible Colombian police Colonel Hugo Rafael Martinez Poveda from the Boyaca Department was placed in charge of Search Bloc's efforts. Selecting a non-Medellin native as leader was crucial for Search Bloc, as the government was deeply paranoid about the intense loyalty toward Pablo that existed in the city. In fact, although Search Bloc ended up numbering around 700 members, not a single one was a native of Medellin or the surrounding area.

So in 1989, Search Bloc was intensifying its hunt, and the United States was throwing more support behind the Colombians than ever before. As a result, the government started to win its first major victories. The deaths of both Jose "The Mexican" Rodriguez Gacha in late 1989 and Pablo's cousin Gustavo Gaviria in 1990 were both attributed to the efforts of the Search Bloc. This intense pressure is what led to Pablo's voluntary surrender in 1991 and his insistence on personal protection while in captivity. Vigilantism was not uncommon in Colombia, and there was no guarantee that rogue Search Bloc members would not still try to assassinate him. But, after Pablo was sent to La Catedral, the military unit largely disbanded. After Pablo escaped from his prison in 1992. though, Search Bloc was rapidly reformed and dispatched once again. The American organizations that were already there, including the DEA, CIA, ATF, FBI, and Delta Force, all stepped up their activities to prevent Pablo from gaining another foothold somewhere. The intelligence service Centra Spike and their cutting edge surveillance technology was instrumental for Search Bloc the first time, and when the search was renewed in 1992, they would again play an incredibly vital role tracking down the elusive cocaine kingpin.

Attacks on Pablo were coming from all sides. Operation Heavy Shadow, the codename for American involvement in the cartel war, was bearing down on him, and the Colombian government had proven they were willing to cooperate even with other drug dealers just to kill Pablo Escobar. The Cali Cartel gave all the support they could to the Search Bloc, and that was in addition to their own attacks on Medellin. Slowly, the center of Colombian drug trafficking power began to shift southwest toward Cali as the Medellin infrastructure started to fracture. Pablo did at least still control much of the city and still had friends despite the fact that he had lost the respect of tens of thousands of Colombians in the past several years. For the time, he had secured a safehouse in the city and was laying as low as possible.

The Search Bloc, aided by the governments of both George Bush and Cesar Gaviria, was fully prepared to track down Pablo across the entire country of Colombia if need be. Indeed, after La Catedral, the search evolved into an absolutely nationwide manhunt. High-ranking politicians, including President Gaviria, were desperate for the peace of mind of having Pablo dead. After Pablo's escape, there was absolutely no telling what the man would do. He had a track record of committing spectacular acts of terror when his back was against the wall, and everyone knew that Pablo was not going to go down quietly. Gaviria had long been fearing for his life because of the death threats he received from The Extraditables, and now he was as afraid as ever. After all, Cesar Gaviria was actually a replacement candidate in the first place, filling in for Luis Carlos Galan who had been assassinated by the cartel back in the summer of 1989. If Pablo could reach Galan, he could certainly reach Gaviria. This was on top of the fact that Pablo was convinced that his cousin Gustavo was slain by the Search Bloc on the direct personal order of President Gaviria. You likely wouldn't have had to look very far down Pablo's hitlist to find the President's name.

So, by the end of 1992, Pablo had become a fugitive once again. The war of terror versus the government was still raging across the country in the major cities like Medellin, Bogota, and Cali, and every enemy that Pablo had made since the early 1970s seemed to be banding together in a united front to finally end the reign of Los Pablos. As the year 1993 approached, another new armed paramilitary group would emerge, also targeting Pablo. This group was in many ways the culmination of years of Pablo's immorality and disregard for human life. They were a brutal, violent vigilante squad that used Pablo's own tactics against him and, being funded by some of the most powerful actors in the state, they ushered in a brand new bloody era of terror across Colombia. This was the most disturbing development for Pablo in years.

Los Pepes And The Fall of Pablo Escobar

When Pablo was first sent to La Catedral in 1991, the Medellin Cartel suffered a rash of defections. Many of their members, fearing that Pablo's organization would effectively buckle under its own weight with the chief imprisoned, decided to get ahead of the game and join up with the rising Cali Cartel instead. Even after Pablo's escape from prison, the bleeding didn't stop, as more and more of his once loyal henchmen abandoned him. Many were opportunistic, looking for better opportunities under new management, but many others simply disagreed with Pablo's years-long campaign of terror, bombing, and public executions. Thousands of Colombian families were being affected by the violence and it all came back to Pablo, the man who grew up in a country plagued by violence and who was now perpetuating it himself. One of the most important men who ditched the Medellin Cartel during these months was a man named Fidel Castano, one of the infamous Castano brothers. Fidel apparently had severe, irreparable grievance against Pablo, and went on to form a terrifying new military group.

To reflect the personal nature of Fidel Castano's vendetta against Pablo, his new group took on the name Los Perseguidos por Pablo Escobar, or in English, "those persecuted by Pablo Escobar." Their members consisted of those who had personal reasons to see the kingpin dead. Some had been financially ruined by him. Some had had their friends and families tortured under his order, and many of them had lost loved ones or close allies. Search Bloc was not the only game in town anymore. Pablo was now being hunted by two separate but related armies, one sanctioned by the government and one vigilante. Unsurprisingly, Castano's group, which came to be popularly known as "Los Pepes," also worked closely with Search Bloc and shared intelligence with them. Because Los Pepes were not an extension of the Colombian government, they had much less oversight and restraint. They used the most vicious methods imaginable to get to Pablo and actively hunted down his family and friends in an attempt to flush him out of hiding.

Fidel Castano apparently had several disagreements with Pablo's leadership that got worse over the years, but it was not until Fidel discovered that Pablo was planning on betraying him that he finally broke away from the Medellin Cartel. Fidel was still a trafficker, though, and at first, he took his talents to the Cali Cartel and began helping them capitalize on Pablo's downfall. After establishing himself with the southwestern traffickers, Fidel's goal pivoted to assassinating his former commander-in-chief. The Cali Cartel chiefs offered their full support for his goal, and even agreed to fund the formation of a military squad for him to command. Los Pepes was birthed soon after, and although many of its conscripts had personal scores to settle with Pablo, they also hired many mercenaries and *sicarios* with paramilitary experience. Many police officers who had their comrades gunned down in the streets and who were disillusioned with the government's progress in stopping Pablo, also joined up with Fidel's group. Many of these officers had open $2,000 contracts still on their heads, courtesy of Pablo Escobar, when they joined. Even members of Colombia's special forces units eagerly enlisted.

Although Los Pepes was not endorsed by the Colombian or American governments, both administrations had an interest in seeing Castano's goals fulfilled. The CIA, an organization with a long and disgusting history of aiding and financing the worst atrocities imaginable, was particularly keen to help Los Pepes get ready for war. The only problem was that the CIA had already gotten themselves in seriously hot water in the 1980s when they were found to have had a role in the infamous Iran-Contra scandal, where American officials were found to have both illegally sold weapons to Iran and used the proceeds from it to illegally fund the bloodthirsty Nicaraguan counter-revolutionary group, the Contras. The Contras had raped and tortured their way through Nicaragua on the CIA's dime, and Los Pepes were hoping to get the same treatment. But they couldn't be caught providing trainings and weapons to what amounted to just another terrorist organization. To get around this legal snag, the CIA worked to encourage more members of Colombian police and special forces to join Los Pepes and then provided training to them only. This dressed up their support of Los Pepes as official government outreach and masked the fact that they were supporting one drug cartel in order to take down another. Los Pepes gunmen even received direct American training on planning assassinations and torturing prisoners. The Cali Cartel, meanwhile, was enjoying the complete ignorance of the American government, and as the Bush administration claimed to be combatting the drug cartels in Colombia, the Cali Cartel continued to pump tons of the powder into America right under their noses.

With Fidel Castano now being funded by the Cali cocaine lords and trained and armed by the American intelligence services, Los Pepes in late 1992 and early 1993 proceeded to conduct one of the most indiscriminate campaigns of terror and death in Colombia's history. Los Pepes targeted literally anyone and everyone who had even the most tangential ties to Pablo Escobar. They wouldn't be satisfied until Pablo was dead, but in the meantime, they were happy to steadily kill everyone else in his life, and as far as Castano was concerned, everyone from Pablo's mother Hermilda down to his casual acquaintances were open game. It was "guilt by association" in the most brutal sense imaginable. Pablo's friends had their homes destroyed and were sent letters threatening the torture of their daughters. Within the space of a few months, Hermilda Escobar had two of her estates torched. Using what they had learned from the CIA (and from the elite Delta Force unit), Los Pepes terrorized the nation and particularly Medellin. Low-level workers at facilities owned by Pablo (even those unrelated to the cocaine business) were abducted and tortured to death. The use of explosives quickly became a trademark of Los Pepes, as the frequency of car bombs and building explosions skyrocketed after they stepped onto the scene.

Pablo Escobar's extensive legal team bore the brunt of Los Pepes' collective fury. In an attempt to cripple him in his numerous legal battles going on in Colombian courts, Los Pepes began targeting cartel lawyers and Pablo's personal attorneys. Any chance that Pablo had of resolving his issues at the Supreme Court level were quickly vanishing as his team members were being routinely abducted and having their lives threatened and homes burned to the ground. In March of 1993, Pablo's chief lawyer in charge of his defense was found dead, and soon after, two more were found the same way. Another lawyer managed to survive his encounter with

Los Pepes but had his family tortured as a consequence. Their brutalist tactics worked quite effectively. In short order, most of Pablo's lawyers who remained alive had resigned and fled the area out of fear for their families' safety. It was clear that Pablo could no longer protect them. The Medellin Cartel boss would now be very hard-pressed to find an attorney in the country who would be willing to represent him—thanks to Los Pepes, Pablo Escobar had become radioactive.

The Medellin Cartel was suffering repeated and heavy losses, but Pablo was not only on the receiving end the state-sponsored violence and vigilante terror. He retaliated against Fidel Castano and the government as brutally as he possibly could, but with the combined onslaught of Los Pepes, Search Bloc, the Colombian state, and the rival Cali Cartel, the most integral structures of the Medellin Cartel had been hamstrung. Pablo simply didn't have the reach that he once did, and it seemed as though the days of him planning audacious and meticulous grand schemes were over. Still, when all you have is a hammer, every problem looks like a nail. Pablo's hammer was bullets and money. In Medellin, police officers were still being mowed down in the street daily, as Pablo continued to pay an open kill contract on every police officer executed in the city. Medellin had turned into a free-for-all murder fest.

While Los Pepes continued their armed suppression of the Medellin Cartel, their Cali counterparts grew their influence more and more, acquiring important contacts within the Gaviria Trujillo administration through bribes and intimidation. And, while Los Pepes marketed themselves as a group fighting for justice for those Pablo Escobar had killed, they had quickly devolved into an opportunistic military wing of the Cali Cartel. They were, in fact, involved in cocaine trafficking and terror just as much as Pablo was. And, as many deaths as Pablo Escobar had caused in recent years, Los Pepes was doing absolutely everything they could to match his numbers. At the height of their violence, Castano's death squads were directly responsible for five murders and executions each and every day on average, all in an effort to force Pablo Escobar out of hiding and into their crosshairs. According to Bowden (2018), over 300 murders in total had been attributed to Los Pepes by the time their campaign concluded at the end of 1993.

Los Pepes were indeed a flat-out terrorist organization, but what was worse was the fact that the Colombian government was almost certainly complicit in all of their activities, including the terrorist attacks. Aside from their direct support from Cali and the United States, President Gaviria's government and the Colombian federal police force also had clear links to the Castano death squads. According to a report in the American National Security Archive (n.d.), the Colombian Police Director Miguel Antonio Gomez "had directed a senior Colombian National Police intelligence to maintain contact with Fidel Castano, paramilitary leader of Los Pepes, and municipal police were willingly providing information to the Los Pepes hitmen. The same document also references prosecutor Gustavo DeGreiff explaining that there was "new, 'very good' evidence linking key members of the police task force in Medellin charged with capturing Pablo Escobar Gaviria [i.e., the Search Bloc] to criminal activities and human rights abuses committed by Los Pepes," but much of this only came to light years later. Clearly, the new vigilante terrorist group was working hand-in-hand with the government of Colombia toward their common goal. This cooperation left a black mark on both the Presidency of Cesar Gaviria as well as the national history of Colombia as a whole.

As far as Pablo was concerned in 1993, it didn't much matter who was funding whom, or where Los Pepes was getting their weapons, or what paramilitary group was in bed with the Americans. All he cared about was that, everywhere he went, his enemies abounded. He continued to fight his war in whatever way he could, delegating orders to those who still remained loyal to him. He was fighting just as he had been in the mid-1980s, but now he wasn't fighting for some principled stance on the constitutionality of extradition. Now, he was fighting just to survive. Like what happened to Carlos Lehder, Pablo's paranoia was beginning to get the better of him, even though Pablo was not helplessly addicted to cocaine like his German-Colombian counterpart). Since 1992, he had become convinced that the attempt to relocate him out of his La Catedral prison resort was in fact a plot to assassinate him planned and sponsored by the Americans. There was almost no one he could trust. He once again tried his hand at making a deal with the Colombian government. He was apparently willing to surrender once again and reenter government custody, but only under the condition that he would not be placed under American supervision where he would surely be executed. Further, he demanded that whatever facility he would be held in be guarded by an impartial and international team of soldiers who could protect him from the American government, the Cali Cartel, and the Los Pepes-Search Bloc military coalition. A family man until the day he died, Pablo also demanded that his relatives be granted safe passage to another country under international protection. Much to his dismay, Pablo discovered quickly that any chance at a negotiated end to his story was long gone.

While Pablo desperately thought of ways to weasel out of his predicament, he was continuing to wage his retaliatory war. Later in 1993, he ordered a massive bomb attack against the Colombian Ministry of Justice. Once again, the kingpin was targeting some of the top politicians and lawmakers in the entire country. Pablo ordered his men to plant a bomb inside a van and drive it up to the Ministry building in Bogota, rigging it to explode right outside of the building's front doors. Unfortunately, like several of Pablo's most recent terror attacks, it ended up being a complete bust. On the day of the attack, Pablo's guys encountered an unusually high level of security on the streets surrounding the Ministry. Realistically, it should not have been a surprise—the government had been learning to anticipate assaults like these for about a decade by this point. As the would-be bombers approached their target, they got nervous at the presence of police and special security. Panicking, the driver turned the van around and left, eventually abandoning it on the curb outside of a nearby bookstore. There, the concealed explosive detonated, instantly killing twenty innocent civilians and causing grievous injury to dozens of others.

The response to the bookstore bombing was resounding, and Pablo's already damaged public image took a fatal hit. Nearly all of the sentimental and principled support he enjoyed from Medellin's public had been destroyed. When Pablo was attacking politicians and rich, exploitative businessmen, he could at least claim that he was fighting for his principles and only against people who deserved it—whether or not this was true. But the car bombing outside of the bookstore, although it was unplanned, came off as pure, blatant terrorism against his fellow Colombians. Combined with the 1989 bombing of Avianca Flight 203, this attack had made him a pariah in the public eye. The government quickly condemned both Pablo and the cartel for the heinous act, and Los Pepes were swift to retaliate. The day after the bookstore explosion, a ranch belonging to Hermilda Gaviria was attacked and razed to the ground, and both Pablo's mother and aunt were badly injured in the assault. The Search Bloc intensified their hunt, and the American agencies poured resources into surveillance technology to assist in the search. A massive $6 million reward was offered to the public in exchange for any information that could lead to Pablo's capture.

At this point, there was almost nowhere in Colombia that Pablo could reliably seek refuge. He was the most notorious criminal in the country, and it didn't matter anymore if he wore the same jeans and t-shirt as everyone else—every Colombian knew his face. As 1993 approached its end, Pablo was getting very scared. He knew that the CIA and their associates were spending millions to survey the country to find him; he also knew that organizations like Centra Spike were pulling 24-hour days to try to use special eavesdropping technology to listen in on his calls and triangulate his location with cell towers. Pablo's anxiety and paranoia were getting worse by the day, and although he outwardly appeared to be the same cold, calculating, and unphased Pablo of the 1970s, he felt his tank running empty. He needed to be able to communicate with his henchmen from within his safehouse if he wanted what remained of his business to continue running, but every time he picked up the phone, he was risking the Search Bloc or Los Pepes discovering his hideout. At one point during the search, Centra Spike team members discovered that Pablo had been using nearly 10 different cell phones in an attempt to throw off his pursuers.

The stress was also taking a physical toll on his body. Pablo had been a bit of a chunky guy since his twenties, but with the never-ending stress, his weight was ballooning and he steadily became obese. Even though he was on "the run," the man barely moved during the day, instead choosing to lay in bed, make his necessary phone and radio calls for the day, and indulge in his marijuana-induced eating binges. Since he decided that the only place he could really hide was in plain sight, he secured a safehouse for himself in Medellin's Los Olivos neighborhood, very close to home. But he could very rarely leave. He feared men with binoculars and recording devices everywhere, which was actually wise of him. As it turned out, Search Bloc was hot on his trail.

On December 2, Pablo was doing his best to celebrate his 44th birthday while in hiding. He couldn't be with his family for obvious reasons, but he did take the risk to call them on the phone. He spoke with his wife and children, and as he did, a squad of Hugo Martinez's men caught the signal from a nearby parking lot where they were monitoring suspected hideouts. The Search Bloc was already pretty confident that he was in the area, but they knew that cordoning off the area and going door-to-door was a mistake— Pablo had proven time and again that he could slither out when backed into a corner, and if he got away this time, he would probably disappear into the jungle. They needed to take their time and be sure of his location, but catching his birthday phone call was a huge development. The most elusive man in Colombia was close by.

The next day, Search Bloc was closing in. They were prepared to mobilize at a moment's notice, and all they were waiting for was confirmation and the go-ahead. Funnily enough, as much high-tech equipment as the American had supplied to Search Bloc, Pablo's location was only confirmed when one of the gunmen visually identified him as he briefly walked by a window in the second story of a house in the middle-class borough of Medellin. Pablo was on the phone, trying to arrange plans for his family to be taken safely out of the country before the Los Pepes madmen got a hold of them. Whatever may be true about Pablo, he was a family man, and he prioritized their safety over his own. Unfortunately, as he tried to save his wife and children, he doomed himself. Once the soldier who spotted him called it in, Search Bloc received the authorization to move in. Their gun squads flew through the city en route to Los Olivos, and within minutes, there was a small army assembled outside of Pablo's safehouse.

The Search Bloc reacted quickly. As they burst forcefully into the house, Pablo went into a panicked rage. He and his bodyguard grabbed their weapons and made a run for it. Colonel Martinez's soldiers unloaded their weapons at the fleeing pair, but they were able to make it to the roof, jumping onto a neighboring rooftop in a desperate attempt to get away. Meanwhile, Pablo was firing blindly behind him, hoping to hit at least a couple of his pursuers. Unsurprisingly, the overweight Pablo had no chance of outrunning the elite, American-trained Search Bloc commandos. They continued their pursuit across the terracotta rooftops, and once they had a clear shot, they unloaded their clips. Pablo's bodyguard already lay dead behind him. The first shot tore through his leg, forcing him down to the ground. Still trying to get away, he received another blow to his back, near his shoulder. The bullet that killed him went into his brain. Pablo Escobar, a former congressman, a prolific terrorist, and the most notorious drug smuggler the world had ever known, was now dead. Search Bloc, the Colombian and American governments, Los Pepes, the Cali Cartel, and the millions affected by his violent spree rejoiced, as his murderers announced over the radio, "Viva Colombia!"

CONCLUSION
THE SUN SETS OVER MEDELLIN

When Pablo first dreamed about escaping poverty and becoming a self-made man, no one could be blamed if they didn't take him seriously. Thousands of poor children from Rionegro had dreams of no longer being the victim of their circumstances, but with the state that their country was in, few were able to make that a reality. Pablo Escobar, on the other hand, meant every word that he said, and when he dedicated himself to something, he always intended to follow through. In the 1970s and 1980s, he followed through in a very big way. Little Pablito had grown into the most successful, most controversial, and most personally fascinating drug lord the world had ever known. He achieved what he set out to do—the man would accumulate more wealth than he could have imagined. The cost, however, ended up being his life, as well as the lives of thousands affected by his drug wars.

A criminal since he was a boy, Pablo eventually built a drug cartel that was powerful enough to challenge the Colombian government itself. He became rich, and he used his wealth to buy influence, which he then used to make himself even richer. It was a vicious cycle that led to Pablo becoming one of the richest and most feared men in the world. He inserted himself into the world of politics, he bought the favor of the poor by showering his charity onto them, and if anyone refused to be swayed, he could have them killed for a pittance. It was a ruthlessly effective system, and everyone in Pablo's mass following was born either out of respect, greed, or fear. The Colombian political body, which Pablo had incessantly terrorized with assassinations, torture, and death threats for years, had little hope of ever curbing his growing power. That is, without the direct and generous support of the American government. It took the collaboration of at least a dozen separate, international organizations, both official and not, to finally bring the man down. But, when he did finally go down, everyone already knew that the city of Medellin and the country of Colombia would never be the same. Neither, for that matter, would the American cities that his cartel flooded with hundreds of tons of cocaine.

The man that built an entire neighborhood for the poor also profited off the suffering of millions. The man that was popular enough to win a seat in Congress also blew up an airplane with over 100 innocent souls aboard. Needless to say, Pablo was a complicated character. Few things can be said for certain about him. He was fiercely loyal to his family. He was a man of his word. And he was also a mass murderer. There is little else at our disposal to paint a clear picture of the man, but his story is nevertheless one of the most fascinating in the world of crime. Even the most eccentric and renowned American mobsters can barely hold a candle to the kind of aura that Pablo Escobar had around him. He was familiar, yet enigmatic. What everyone did know was that, in late 1993, the man was finally dead, and it was time to move on. But how could they? Could it really be so simple to forget about a man who literally altered the fabric of day-to-day Colombian life?

Indeed, his death was still considered a tragedy by many. Even though his acts of terror in the late 1980s and early 1990s tarnished his previously godly reputation among Medellin's lower classes, he was still mourned. Over 20,000 people attended his funeral, and many openly wept for him. Elsewhere, people rejoiced. As many admirers as he had, he had twice as many enemies. Countless families had lost loved ones, and they blamed him. The Americans celebrated a historic victory in the so-called War on Drugs, despite the fact that the Cali Cartel was rapidly becoming Colombia's premiere cocaine gang. The balance of power had begun to shift toward the city of Cali soon after Pablo was forced to go on the run upon escaping La Catedral. Once the kingpin was dead, the Medellin infrastructure crumbled and the center of Colombia's drug industry dramatically swung to the southwest.

Even with the rise of a new generation of drug lords, none are remembered as closely as Pablo Escobar. After his death, his grand Hacienda Napoles luxury estate was retrofitted and turned into something of an amusement park. To this day, it remains a popular tourist attraction and national landmark. It still contains much of what Pablo himself had installed (at least, everything that hadn't been confiscated or destroyed by the police), and it serves as a clear reminder of the sheer grandeur of his life. Documentaries, fictionalized television shows, and blockbuster movies are still being made about his life and the lives of those around him, serving as a testament to his everlasting allure. Of all the accounts of his life and his career depicted in media, though, there is only one clear lesson to be taken: Pablo's wealth and power just could not save him in the end. Pablo's cartel, at its height, was bringing in hundreds of millions of American dollars every single week from flooding cities like Miami and Los Angeles. He had more power and influence than any one man should have, but when he finally went down, he died just like a common criminal—shot down in public by the law.

REFERENCES

Attwood, S. (2016). *Pablo Escobar: Beyond Narcos.* Gadfly Press.

Bowden, M. (2016, August 14). *Killing Pablo.* Atlantic Books.

Escobar, J. P. (2016, August 30). *Pablo Escobar: My father.* Thomas Dunne Books.

Farah, D. (1998, August 29). In Colombia, Marlboro country is smugglers' haven. *The Washington Post.* https://www.washingtonpost.com/archive/politics/1998/08/30/in-colombia-marlboro-country-is-smugglers-haven/55f39f47-4552-47cc-87d0-160d0f78975b/

Frontline: The godfather of cocaine script. (n.d.). PBS.org. https://www.pbs.org/wgbh/frontline/wgbh/pages/frontline/programs/transcripts/1309.html

Hearings before the Permanent Subcommittee on Investigations of the Committee on Governmental Affairs, United States Senate. (1989, September 12-13). Office of Justice Programs. https://www.ojp.gov/pdffiles1/Digitization/146771NCJRS.pdf

Legarda Martínez, A. (2017, November 24). *The true life of Pablo Escobar: Blood, betrayal, and death.* Ediciones y Distribuciones Dipon, ltda.

Long, W. (1989, December 7). Bogota blast kills 45; drug kingpins blamed : Colombia: Bus bomb rips through the headquarters of the police intelligence agency. 400 are injured. *The Los Angeles Times.* https://www.latimes.com/archives/la-xpm-1989-12-07-mn-253-story.html

Micolta, P. (2012). *Illicit interest groups: The political impact of the Medellin drug trafficking organizations in Colombia.* Florida International University. https://digitalcommons.fiu.edu/cgi/viewcontent.cgi?article=1732&context=etd

The Palace of Justice siege. (n.d.). Center of Justice and Accountability. https://cja.org/what-we-do/litigation/palace-of-justice/

Smith, H. (2018, December 10). Belisario Betancur, Colombian president who led unsuccessful peace effort, dies at 95. *The Washington Post.* https://www.washingtonpost.com/local/obituaries/belisario-betancur-colombian-president-who-led-unsuccessful-peace-effort-dies-at-95/2018/12/10/d7da8664-fc8f-11e8-862a-b6a6f3ce8199_story.html

Walsh, P. (1984, November 26). *A car bomb exploded Monday outside the U.S. embassy,...* UPI.com. https://www.upi.com/Archives/1984/11/26/A-car-bomb-exploded-Monday-outside-the-US-Embassy/8994470293200/

Woody, C. (2016, August 8). *Two guys in a Connecticut jail cell helped change the way America does drugs.* Business Insider.

https://www.businessinsider.com/carlos-lehder-george-jung-prison-cell-together-drug-trafficking-plans-2016-8

Woody, C. (2022, December 3). *Pablo Escobar was gunned down 29 years ago — here are 3 theories about who took the Medellin kingpin's life.* Business Insider. https://www.businessinsider.com/who-killed-notorious-colombian-drug-kingpin-pablo-escobar-2016-12